CLIMBING
TERMS & TECHNIQUES

CLIMBING
TERMS & TECHNIQUES
KEN CROCKET

First published in 1990

British Library Cataloguing in
Publication Data
Crocket, Ken, *1948-*
  Climbing terms and
  techniques.
  1. Climbing. Techniques
  I. Title
  796.5'22

This edition published
1993 by Fraser Stewart
Book Wholesale Limited,
Abbey Chambers,
4 Highbridge Street,
Waltham Abbey,
Essex EN9 1DQ

Produced by the promotional
Reprint Company Limited, UK.

ISBN 1-85648-157-3

Printed in Finland by WSOY

Disclaimer

While every attempt has been made to ensure that the advice and suggestions given in this book will be appropriate for the 'normal' individual in the situations described, neither author nor publisher can accept any responsibility for accidents or injury, however sustained, in the course of climbing activities. As with any potentially dangerous physical pastime readers are reminded that safety is ultimately the responsibility of participating individuals. At the same time sensible precautions and reasonable consideration for the rights and safety of others go a long way towards fostering goodwill amongst climbers and non-climbers alike.

Acknowledgements

Thanks are due to the climbing friends with whom I have enjoyed the mountains. In the preparation of this book Alastair Walker was a willing model and climbing partner. Graham Truscott, Senior Editor at Patrick Stephens, was a pleasure to work with. Finally, thanks are due to the generosity of the following local mountaineering retailers who lent equipment; Highrange Sports, Nevisport, Tiso.

Introduction

The increasing amount and complexity of climbing equipment over the last decade has brought problems along with the benefits. No amount of shiny, high-tech alloy hung on a harness will help anyone unless properly used, and there lies the problem. Faced with a limited budget and limited experience what should be the priority purchases? What to buy and how to use it? Climbing days are short and far between and experienced friends may be hard to find. Whatever your standard of climbing you may wish to try a new climbing technique or to improve on an existing one. It is my hope and intention that reading the relevant page the night before could save you much time, and more.

You may never have to use some of the techniques explained in this book. Some, indeed, you will go out of your way to avoid! Bad weather may break at any time, however, crevasses yawn unseen on a glacier crossing, while some tempting items of equipment might be of better use in the kitchen than on the crag. All of the terms and techniques you are likely to need for safe and competent climbing are explained here. I have tried to link clear and concise words to clear and simple diagrams where an illustration could be helpful. Equipment described for use in the various techniques is in common use today. Although some of the items mentioned are of very recent manufacture, they have been tried out during the writing of this book. Complicated and unnecessary rope tricks are avoided.

The best years of climbing, in retrospect, are often the early ones. Every route is a new and exciting adventure. Beginnings, however, are also very often a hazardous time, and many an older, grizzled climber has a collection of climbing frights gathered during inexperienced explorations. The excitement of the sport should remain as a climber gains experience, but experienced climbers often forget some of the finer points of technique, content to continue with accustomed habits, bad or otherwise. There should be useful reading here for them too. During my formative years I gained confidence and knowledge from a good techniques book: used as an accessory to hands-on training it can only improve your climbing.

Finally, while the terms and techniques shown here will be acceptable to most climbers, equipment and methods evolve. I would be delighted to hear comments from readers on any point, sending suggestions via the publisher in the first instance.

Terms and techniques

Abseil. To descend rapidly by sliding down a rope. Often necessary in the Alps when caught by bad weather on a route, or as a convenient way of fast descent following an ascent (which seems to be growing in popularity as a technique). Normally uses the standard two climbing *ropes* of 9mm diameter, tied together by a *double fisherman's knot* and running through an *abseil loop* attached to a *belay* point such as a *peg* or *sling* round a rock spike. Using a single rope would immediately half the possible length of abseil. To increase control, friction is increased by running the ropes through a device such as a *figure-of-eight* which in turn is attached to the climber's *harness*. The lower ends of the ropes are best tied together in a lumpy knot, to prevent abseiling off the ends by mistake.

After securing the anchor and attaching the abseil ropes, carefully throw the loops down and out from the face, avoiding snagging the ropes. In a high wind it may be necessary to attach a little weight to the ends, such as a couple of heavy *karabiners*. Double check all points of attachment and the path of the ropes before starting an abseil. Slowly walk backwards over the edge, with the rear, lower hand controlling the rate of rope movement. The upper hand is mainly used for balance or perhaps

sliding down a safety *prusik*. A steady descent minimizes stress on the anchor point. Leave the heroic, and unnecessary bouncy descents to the

Abseil

1. *Climber is abseiling using a Dulfer sit sling, in the semi-classic, rope-over-the-shoulder method. In the true classic style, with no sit sling, the ropes would run between the legs before coming back up and over one shoulder. The feet should be used, where possible, to steady the descent.*

Abseil

2. *Using a Dulfer sit sling in the semi-classic method. The right hand, in this example, is the controlling hand, with a twist of rope taken round the wrist to increase the friction. The other hand is used for balance.*

3. *Details of abseil method using a Dulfer sit sling.*

stunt men. Avoid running the ropes over sharp edges or into cracks which might jam the ropes irretrievably. Think twice before swinging to a new descent line; if the rope is running over a sharp edge above it can cut through in seconds. Once a safe stance and new anchor have been gained by abseil, the ropes are collected by pulling on the side with the knot (which will be lower than the anchor), the other side then running smoothly up to and through the anchor. Remember which colour of rope has to be pulled before starting the abseil. The first climber down should test that the ropes can be recovered by gently pulling on the down rope (but don't let go of the other rope!)

The climbers' nightmare begins when the ropes refuse to pull through, jamming somewhere above. If both ends of the rope are at hand and the anchor above is definitely secure, it is possible to prusik up (using both ropes of course) and sort out the problem, though this will be both strenuous and time-consuming. If the rope has already partly passed through the anchor above then jammed so that only one end is available we have a serious situation, best alleviated by waving for attention from other parties. On no account begin climbing up using the rope: your life quality will be radically altered.

Abseiling is also increasingly used in rock climbing to inspect and clean prospective *new routes* or examine very difficult pitches before an attempt. The list of good mountaineers killed during abseiling is a depressingly long one, and the technique is at best hazardous. Most experienced climbers have their bad abseil story. If worried by the quality of the anchor and a spare rope is at hand then the first climber down can

Abseil

4. Abseiling using a figure-of-eight descender and a harness. The ropes are in the descent, or fast position, as they have a small turning angle and decreased friction through the descender.

5. Abseiling using a figure-of-eight descender and a harness. The ropes are in the locking, or slow position, as the turning angle has been increased by bringing down the controlling rope.

be belayed by a safety rope using a separate belay. Common causes of accident during abseil include failure of the anchor, loss of control, clothing or equipment jamming the ropes, abseiling off the ends of the ropes, or being hit by stonefall perhaps caused by the ropes.

An abseil can also be safeguarded by attaching a prusik loop to the ropes. In the event of a sudden, uncontrolled descent, this might lock and stop a fall, though it will slow down an abseil and is another complication in itself. To abseil by the classic method is to do so with neither harness nor, obviously, friction device. This is even more hazardous and very uncomfortable, the ropes being passed between the legs, up across the front of the body, over the opposite shoulder. It will be needed only if no harness or sling is available. If a sling is handy make a *sit sling* out of it and use a karabiner to run the ropes through. Practise abseiling on a short outcrop with a safety rope held by a companion and regard it as a necessary but potentially dangerous technique.

Abseil

6. *Abseil with figure-of-eight descender and harness. In order to stop and free the hands. perhaps to arrange a belay, the climber has taken several turns of the ropes round one thigh, locking the rope. Another way would be to use a short prusik loop attached to the harness.*

Abseil loop. A short length of nylon cord used to attach the abseil ropes to the anchor. The anchor is usually a peg, jammed *chockstone*, or sling attached to a flake or chockstone, and the most commonly used loop is 7mm kernmantel. If the anchor is a natural feature such as a rock spike then tubular tape may be more convenient, lying flat on the rock and more easily slipped down behind a flake. To avoid leaving a karabiner the loop is untied until threaded through the eye of a secure peg, retying it with a *double fisherman's knot*. In an emergency, however, gear is much cheaper than one's life, and there should be no hesitation over leaving pegs, slings, karabiners, nuts etc in order to safeguard a hazardous situation.

Acclimatization. The gradual adaptation to high altitude; necessary over about 4000m for most climbers. The effects of going too high too soon are caused by the lower oxygen content of the air at increased heights. Himalayan expeditions typically have an approach march stage, allowing natural changes in physiology to occur, such as an increase in the red blood cell count. The effects can be felt as low as about 3000m, with headaches, sleeplessness and nausea typical signs. More serious is *altitude sickness*, which can lead to pulmonary or cerebral oedema, with water collecting in the lungs or brain. The only cure is a rapid removal to lower altitude.

A cheval. From the French 'on horseback', and a technique of climbing a ridge or easy-angled *arête* with a leg down each side and hands on the ridge. A shuffling series of moves, alternating hands and feet, makes for safe, if clumsy progress.

Active rope. The second man, belaying the *leader*, passes the rope or double rope through a belaying device. The side of the rope towards the leader is the active or 'live' rope, while the side of the rope on the far side of the belaying device will be held by the second's 'controlling' hand. Should the leader fall, the all-important controlling hand, which must never be taken off the rope while belaying, will do the necessary movement to lock the rope in the belaying device. Normally, a rapid arm movement across the body and towards the falling climber will increase the angle through which the ropes turn in the belaying device, thus increasing the friction and locking the ropes. See *belay* and *belay plate*.

Aid climbing. To make a move, or series of moves on a climb, with the physical assistance of equipment is to use aid. This could be as simple as resting or pulling on a runner or, on very steep and smooth rock to make continuous movement using pegs, bolts etc in conjunction with short nylon ladders of two to four rungs called *étriers*. A *cow's tail* may be used: a short length of accessory cord connected to the harness can be clipped into a peg to allow both hands to be free and provide a rest. Very hard climbs may have several such aid points and yet be recognized as intrinsically free routes; beyond this level of assistance the route becomes an aid route or a route with an aid pitch. There is much healthy controversy over the use of bolts on otherwise free routes, where they may be used for fixed points of protection in situations where protection is poor or absent. Aid climbing in the UK enjoyed a brief popularity in the '50s and '60s. In the United States many advances in the design of pegs are owed to the giant aid routes on Yosemite Valley's granite walls.

Aiguilles. Rock needles which may be quite large, as in the case of well-known landmarks such as the Aiguille du Dru on the Mont Blanc range.

Alcohol. a) Used as a pre-heater for paraffin *stoves*, in the form of methylated spirits, or for cooking using an alcohol stove.
b) Abuse of drinking alcohol, as in any other sport, will drastically reduce your ability and even create a hazard. If climbing the next day moderate your intake the night before. If you climb under the influence of alcohol then you have a problem.

Alp. In the true sense of the word, and as used in the European Alps, an alp is the high, grassy slope between the valley and the snowline, used by locals as a summer pasture. Early travellers used it to refer to the entire mountain, hence its modern use as meaning an entire mountain range such as the Alps.

Alpenstock. A precursor to the ice axe, being a long pole with a metal spike at the lower end. Used by early mountaineers for glacier travel and on easy snow slopes until about the 1870s.

Alpine climbing. Normally taken to mean climbing in the European Alps at high altitude; above the snow line. Such climbers are then Alpinists. Also climbing at altitude anywhere in the world. The differences between Alpine climbing and climbing done at lower altitudes is often one of effort. Distances will be longer, routes longer. A rucksack will often have to be worn on a route. Big boots may be worn for convenience and, on a *mixed route*, through necessity. *Bivouac* gear may need to be carried, so that the rucksack is heavier. The effects of altitude may lower your performance: even a headache, induced perhaps by the altitude or some drastic early start, may be enough. Fitness will cure most of these obstacles, with a good all-round ability on rock and ice being the underlying key to safe climbing and the opportunity to enjoy the higher mountain ranges of the world.

Alpine fashion. See *moving together*.

Alpine start. In the Alps above the snow line it is important to cross any snow while it is in good condition, ie, hard. As the day warms the snow obviously softens, not only making progress irksome, but increasing the danger of avalanche. When traversing a *glacier* too it is safer when the snow is hard, as hidden *crevasses* may often be crossed in safety. To avoid soft snow, a climbing party may leave a hut or *bivouac* and approach the chosen route well before dawn, perhaps just after midnight when a long day is planned. *Headtorches* may be required. An Alpine start is not everyone's favourite, but in compensation the route should be safer and quieter, while dawn is always welcome.

Altitude sickness. See *acclimatization*.

Andesite. A volcanic rock named after its type location in the South American Andes Mountains. Ben Nevis is formed of andesite, which is a fine-grained, dark rock, usually formed as lava flows. Other climbing areas with andesite include Glencoe and the Lake District.

Aneroid. An aneroid barometer can be useful on a long Alpine route in giving an approximate indication of altitude. It should be set at the beginning of the day when at a known height. It can also warn of approaching bad weather as it will then indicate a drop in barometric pressure. High wind can effect the reading, increasing the local pressure.

Anorak. Developed from the original Inuit (Eskimo) garment this protective jacket is usually made of nylon, is waterproof and windproof, has a hood, full length front zip, pockets, and adjustable wrist cuffs. The hood can be tightened with built-in drawcords and there may be an internal waist cord to further protect the wearer from the elements. In the 1970s DuPont Chemicals developed a nylon called Gore-Tex which can be incorporated in an anorak as a thin layer, formed as a laminate between two layers of conventional material. It has a large number of very small pores which allow water vapour to escape but prevents the ingress of water droplets. In practice the wearer is more comfortable as water vapour due to perspiration will not build up to the same extent as in a conventional nylon anorak. There are now other nylons on the market aspiring to the same end, while the traditional waxed cotton jackets do the same job at least as well, if more heavily.

Arête. The narrow crest of a mountain ridge, often giving spectacular walking or climbing. It can vary in angle from the horizontal to the vertical.

Artificial climbing. See *aid climbing*.

Artificial climbing wall. Somewhat confusingly, this has nothing to do with *aid climbing*, but is a man-made wall designed and built to allow climbing practice. Most of the major British cities have climbing walls of some sort. Their immediate precursor is a man-made wall not specifically built for climbing but providing good training. Railway walls in particular seemed to have been designed by incipient climbers. Good artificial climbing walls will have a variety of problems such as overhangs, pillars, walls etc, with various shapes and sizes of holds in place. A soft mat below the wall, which rarely exceeds 6m in height, permits a safe landing if soloing, though walls should have *top-rope* facilities. They allow a high standard of climbing to be gained and maintained, particularly over the winter months when rock climbing outdoors may be difficult. Not all walls are indoors. Concrete is a common material, with many good walls having holds of natural rock embedded in the matrix. See *training*.

Ascender. A device allowing a climber to climb or *prusik* up a fixed rope. The device, which may be mechanical or a knot specifically designed for this purpose, is easily slid up the rope by the climber but under load tightens on the rope, preventing downward movement. Normally ascenders are used in pairs, with the lower used in conjunction with a foot loop, and the upper attached to the climbing *harness*. The basic ascender is made by tying a *prusik knot* in 5mm rope (for use with a 9mm main rope), or in 7mm rope, if using an 11mm main rope. A compromise is to use 6mm accessory cord which will work on both diameters of main rope. It is important that the prusik rope be thinner than the climbing rope to which it will be attached, in order that it tightens adequately under load, gripping the climbing rope.

There are at least six other knots or variations of knots which are designed for ascending, some incorporating a *karabiner* as a convenient hand grip, and also several mechanical ascenders, of which the most familiar name is the *jumar*. Mechanical devices often have left and right-hand units, and are suitable for expedition work or routes demanding much prusiking. See *jumar*. The prusik knot can fail if used in wet conditions, on a muddy rope, or if subjected to shock loading such as in a short fall. It can also jam. On the plus side it can, with practice, be tied with one hand, which might be useful in certain emergencies. Using a prusik knot with a karabiner provides a handhold and lessens the chances of the knot jamming.

A better knot for ascending a rope is the *klemheist*, particularly when finished with a *sheet bend*. The klemheist is less prone to jamming. Whichever knot is used for ascending a rope, be aware that a sudden fall may be fatal, as the knot can then slip without tightening. There have been fatalities through solo climbers using a prusik knot for *self-protection*. Guard against this by tying an *overhand* knot at regular intervals in the slack rope beneath, preferably at short intervals. It will slow progress but is infinitely better than falling off the end of the rope. (There should also be a bulky knot at the end of the rope, for the same preventive purpose.) Situations where prusiking may be necessary include recovery of a jammed abseil rope, *self-rescue* after a fall on a route or into a *crevasse*, and prusiking up a fixed rope for route cleaning or inspection, on an expedition or major, multi-day route.

Avalanche. The sudden downward movement of a mass of snow, ice or rock. Most commonly of snow and during, or shortly following, heavy snowfall. Also common during a thaw. Snow can avalanche at a surprisingly low slope angle, and indeed the zone of greatest danger lies with slopes of between 30 and 45 degrees. There are three basic type of avalanche:
a) Wet-snow avalanche. As the name implies this will be found at higher temperatures; during a thaw or in heavy snowfall at or above freezing levels. This type of avalanche is particularly dangerous as the snow often becomes very hard on coming to a halt, trapping victims. Avoidable for the most part, as dangerous conditions are usually obvious. Apart from the amount of snow falling, and the high temperature, small slides of snow with 'snowballs' running down slopes spontaneously should persuade even the highest risk-taker that it's time to abandon ship.
b) Dry-snow avalanche. In colder conditions loose powder snow may not be able to attach to underlying material, sliding off easily. Gullies

will have almost continuous flows of *spindrift* in certain conditions, smaller amounts of dry snow which, though uncomfortable, may not be heavy enough to be dangerous. More dangerous are the large, open-slope powder avalanches, which particularly in the Alps can be very large, fast and devastating. In big examples, the high-velocity wind in front of such an avalanche may blow down trees. Snow can be driven into the lungs, killing quickly by asphyxiation.

c) Wind-slab avalanche. Given certain conditions, with falling snow being packed in by high winds, a layer of reasonably firm snow can form on top of an underlying layer of more loose snow, to which it is not firmly joined. This upper slab of snow can then fracture and break off, often triggered by the victim walking over the surface. Though not immediately obvious, there are warning signs which can help avoid this type of avalanche. The slab often 'creaks' underfoot, and small areas can break away with a climber's foot breaking through the crust. A *snow profile*, digging a hole down through the layers, can confirm the presence of windslab.

If unfortunate enough to be caught in an avalanche, common (and sensible) advice is to attempt to stay on the surface, avoid breathing in snow, and make a space around yourself as the avalanche comes to a halt. Though there have been amazing cases of survival following burial, the odds are poor. If you survive the immediate avalanche, find the other victims and resuscitate if necessary. As over half of buried victims will be dead within thirty minutes, it is hardly worth going for help, unless of course there is a spare person available. Search for victims immediately, if safe to do so. Skiers can carry electronic devices allowing them to

Bachmann knot

Used as a friction knot. The karabiner makes it easier to hold and slide up a rope. The number of turns round the rope may be varied according to circumstances and the amount of friction needed.

be quickly found if buried; before these were invented avalanche cords were trailed behind the skier, 30m lengths of brightly-coloured cord marked with arrows pointing in the direction of the skier. See *first aid*.

Bachar ladder. See *training*.

Bachmann knot. A sliding friction knot useful for prusiking and pulley systems. Superior to the *prusik* knot as it is less likely to jam after loading and holds better on wet or icy ropes. Requires both hands for tying and is conveniently used in conjunction with a *karabiner*. This provides a good hold giving less hand fatigue, and makes it easier to slide up a rope. The amount of friction can be varied by altering the number of turns.

Back bearing. A navigation technique using a *compass* which can help fix one's position if momentarily lost or unsure. It requires at least two identifiable and visible landmarks. Take compass *bearings* on each land-

mark and allow for *magnetic variation*. Add or subtract 180 degrees, depending on whether the bearings are less or greater than 180 degrees. These two back bearings, when drawn from the landmarks, should cross at your position. See *bearing*.

Backing up. Also known as back and foot. A rock climbing technique allowing narrow *chimneys* to be climbed. In an ideal situation the climber has his or her back against one wall, and feet against the opposing wall. Moving up is done by alternately pushing up with the hands on the back wall and moving the feet further up the opposing wall, relying on friction and any holds. If the chimney is narrower then knees may also come into use.

Back rope. A method used to protect a *second* on a *traverse*, where a fall could result in a dangerous swing. Useful for a weak second or a potentially dangerous traverse with poor rock, great *exposure* and so on. A *runner* is placed at the start of the traverse. If, as is common, two ropes are in use, one is run through the runner, with the other rope leading directly to the belayed leader. As the second makes the traverse towards the *belay*, the leader takes in the direct rope as normal but carefully pays out the other rope through the runner. Any fall while traversing should be very limited. After traversing, the back rope is untied from the second and pulled through the runner, unless a spike has been used, in which case it might be possible to lift it off with a flicking motion.

Balaclava. A head covering, originally woollen, covering head and neck, with an oval 'window' for the face. Developed during the Crimean War and giving excellent protection in winter conditions. Thinner ones

---

Backing up

Here the technique is used to climb a wide chimney, with back against one wall and feet against the opposing wall. One hand is usefully pushing down on an edge hold.

Bandolier

An alternative way of carrying equipment is the over-the-shoulder bandolier. Protection gear is, in this example, graded on the bandolier, with big chockstones and Friends to the front, and small chockstones, wires etc to the rear.

of forces and movements while climbing. This can range from walking over rough ground to climbing up steep rock or ice. A balance move in climbing is one made without a positive handhold, such as when moving up a rock slab relying on foot friction and with hands maintaining equilibrium only and not pulling up or in. Except on steeper rock, balance climbing is the normal way of moving, and is much less strenuous than over-reliance on arm strength. Balance climbing also applies in winter climbing, allowing steeper slopes to be climbed with less effort, using the spike or pick of an *ice axe* as an extension to the hand.

Balling up. See *crampons*.

Bandolier. Nylon sling or stiffened nylon band worn over the shoulder and used for attaching *protection* equipment: *runners, karabiners* etc. Part of the bandolier is broad for comfort, part narrow, to allow karabiners to be easily clipped in. Some climbers find the gear loops on *harnesses* too low, with the possibility of runners catching on rocks when descending. The bandolier raises equipment slightly higher, and also allows a complete gear *rack* to be quickly passed over to another climber.

Barometer. See *aneroid*.

Basalt. Volcanic rock, variable in quality but often weathering easily and then providing poor climbing rock. Commonly found as vertical dykes or horizontal sills, cutting through older basement rocks through which it has been intruded. These dykes often weather to form chimneys or gullies.

made from silk or nylon fit conveniently under a climbing *helmet*. It can also be used as a hat, rolled up into itself.

Balance. A fine awareness of the position of one's body and the effects

Base camp. The main encampment on a climbing trip requiring the use

Bearing

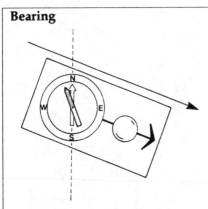

1. *Place one of the long edges of the compass along the desired direction of travel. Rotate the compass dial so that N and S align with the NS grid lines on the map. Take the reading off the dial (in this example, 110 degrees, just south of East).*

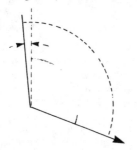

2. *As the Earth's magnetic pole 'wanders' about from year to year, most maps will give an indication of the necessary correction to be made. In the UK, it will be about 6 degrees West, so add this amount, giving a reading of 116 degrees.*

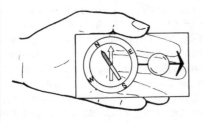

3. *Rotate the dial to read 116 degrees against the direction of travel arrow. Rotate your body and with it the compass, until the magnetic needle points to North, then follow the direction of travel arrow.*

of tents for mobility and convenience. There may, as in Himalayan expedition work, be higher camps, with base camp used for rest periods. On the lower heights, a base camp may be used on a daily basis, climbers returning to it after a day's climbing.

Bearing. When navigating by map and compass in mist or over strange land it will be necessary at some point or points to take a bearing, which will be a number, in degrees, to be followed for some distance or until a landmark is reached. The modern 'Silva' or 'Suunto' type compass makes this task easier. The compass is basically a transparent perspex rectangle on which is mounted a rotating dial. The dial contains a freely balanced magnetic needle damped by a viscous liquid. A prominent arrow is also marked on the base of the rotating dial, while there is a direction of travel arrow on the rectangle, parallel to the edges.

To follow a bearing from one point on a map to the next, line up one long edge of the rectangle parallel to the required route. Without moving the rectangle on the map rotate the dial until the arrow on the base of the dial (which is also North, or zero degrees on the outside of the dial) points in the same direction as the grid lines on the map, with north pointing to the north, or top, of the map. The compass can now be removed from the map for the final stages. First, make an adjustment for magnetic north, which at this time is about 5 or 10 degrees west of grid north in the British Isles. (Check the map for the amount and direction). If magnetic variation is to the west, then add the necessary number of degrees by rotating the dial, otherwise subtract. Finally, hold the compass level and swivel around so that the magnetic needle coincides with

North on the outside of the dial. Walk in the direction parallel to the edge of the compass rectangle, as indicated by the direction of travel indicator, keeping the magnetic needle coincident with North on the dial.

In poor visibility on featureless ground, it may be necessary to use a companion as a temporary target, some distance in front (not too far!). The compass needle should have luminous points, to facilitate night navigation, and must be attached to the owner with a cord, to prevent it being lost in a gale. The art of good navigation, unsurprisingly, is not to get lost in the first place. One common error is to dutifully take a bearing from some summit but not follow it for the necessary distance during descent.

Belay. Belaying includes the techniques and equipment necessary to safely attach a climber to a slope. A wide variety of gear is available for both summer and winter, with a good working knowledge and understanding of proper belaying being essential for safe climbing. (The use of the word belay is slowly settling to mean what was once called a static belay, ie, one to which the belaying climber would be attached while the other climber was moving. The dynamic, or running belay, attached at intervals on a section of climb or pitch for protection by the leader, is now generally called a runner. These will be the terms used here.)

The best belay, summer or winter, is probably a full strength nylon *sling* hung round a secure rock flake or spike, preferably so that it will not easily be lifted off in any direction. A *karabiner* on the belay sling is then used to tie on the ropes. The sling should be long enough to reduce the turning angle and maximize its strength. A *figure-of-eight knot* is nor-

Belay

1. *A good, solid flake is used here for a belay. A long sling round the flake reduces the turning angle and maximizes the strength. The climbing rope is tied into a screwgate karabiner using a figure-of-eight knot.*

Note that the connecting sling will help prevent the chockstone from falling out of its placement.

mally used to attach the ropes to the karabiner. This knot is easily learned and tied, is secure, and fairly easily untied even after a loading. An alternative knot, quickly tied, is the *clove hitch*, though when using a double rope it is impractical to tie both ropes into the same karabiner. The best slings for main belays are stitched supertapes, 2.4m in length, 25mm wide. These are carried, shortened for convenience into a figure-of-eight loop and with a karabiner through both loops, over one shoulder, and each rope of two climbers should have at least two. Also useful for belays and full-strength runners are the same tapes in 1.2m lengths.

These tapes are machine-stitched in the factory, giving a strong, permanent and low profile join; don't even contemplate trying to emulate this on an ordinary domestic sewing machine. The breaking strength of a 25mm, 1.2m standard Troll tubular tape sling is 2000kg. One interesting development in ropes is *Kevlar*. See *kernmantel* for more information on this.

Other methods of belaying include the use of artificial *nuts* or *chockstones*, made of aluminium alloys in a wide range of shapes and sizes. Larger nuts are used with nylon slings; the

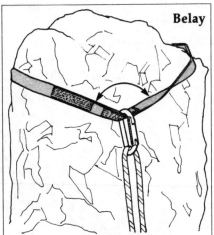

Belay

3. *A too-short sling on a flake. The turning angle is too great, reducing its strength. Use a longer sling, or connect two together.*

smaller nuts are sold already mounted with swaged wire. A development from rocks and stones jammed in conveniently sized cracks, which led to industrial nuts with drilled-out threads, nuts are being constantly researched and improved. One basic rule remains however — the bigger the nut the better. A large, well-placed nut will be as strong as the main rope. When using a nut for a main belay remember that a belayer may well be pulled from above as well as below. It is therefore good insurance to have more than one anchor point at a belay, and to try to allow for forces from any direction. Two nuts in opposition, for example, are much better than one. The same philosophy can hold for the placement of runners, though here additional safety must be balanced against too much time spent in artistic runner arranging. See *protection*.

Short nut slings, when used for either a main belay or a runner, can cause bad rope *drag* by forcing the main rope down over an edge or holding it in a crack. This should be

Belay

2. *The climber has improved the belay by tying into an opposed chockstone. The chockstone is placed so as to hold an upward pull, the weak point with the flake sling. This should be a 'bombproof' belay. The ropes are passing through a belay plate, connected to the harness via a separate screwgate karabiner, and the climber is ready to take in or pay out the ropes to the other climber.*

Belay

4. *A good peg belay. A Cassin Lost Arrow being positioned in a horizontal crack. About two thirds of the peg is pushed down into the crack.*

avoided by using an extension sling and another karabiner. These extension slings, known also as *extenders* and quick draws, are either standard tape loops or special shock absorbing types. If standard tape they are best bought stitched, otherwise buy as a length and knot using a *tape knot*. They are usually shorter than belay slings, from about 10 to 25cm in doubled length, and 12 to 25mm width. Shock absorbing tapes have been stitched so that in the event of a fall, stitches will be gradually ripped out, lengthening the sling and absorbing some of the energy. They cost more than standard tape. Most of the energy of a fall will be absorbed by the climbing rope, and here it is worth mentioning that the properties of the main rope are different from accessory cord in that climbing rope has much more extensibility than accessory cord. For this reason do not be tempted to buy and use long lengths of accessory cord. They are not suitable for use as a climbing rope, even for *top roping*.

The use of *pegs* for belays is now mostly confined to winter and Alpine climbing. In the Alps many pegs will be found in situ, especially on the popular routes. They should always be treated with caution, though they will probably be longer-lasting than tape and rope slings. Many abseil belays will be pegs, often with an interesting and colourful collection of sun-faded *abseil loops*. These loops, exposed to the weather and especially UV radiation, gradually lose their strength; they may be physically abraded as well. Depending on the number and condition of loops on a belay, either use with caution or leave a new sling behind. Pegs should be placed so as to best oppose potential pulls. A horizontal crack is generally

Belay

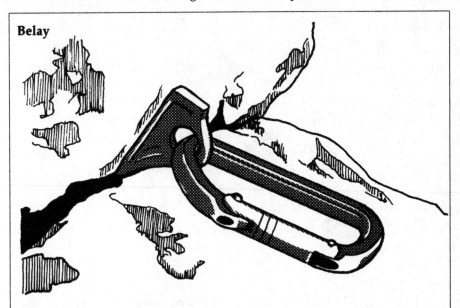

5. Cassin Lost Arrow peg hammered home in a horizontal crack, and with a karabiner attached.

6. Using a Deadman belay in snow. Dig a trench across the slope and a thin slot at right angles down from the middle of the trench, to accommodate the cable. The trench and slot should meet like a 'T'.

Belay

7. The deadman is now placed at an angle of about 40 degrees to the uphill slope. If necessary hammer it home by hitting the reinforcing bar.

8. Finally, pull down on the cable, keeping it parallel to the slope. The belay ledge should be below the end of the cable.

the best choice. The quality of a peg placement can often be measured by the sound as it is hammered home, with a steadily rising pitch being good.

In winter, rock features may be found and used as in summer, except that snow and ice will often obscure. To compensate, three additional

belay methods may be used. Snow or ice *bollards* can be amongst the most secure of belay anchors, depending on the conditions. With good ice, cut a bollard measuring about 50cm in diameter, with a narrow trench of about a hand's-length in depth round about it, shape on the uphill side so

Belay

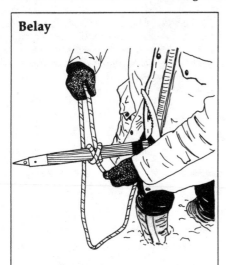

9. Buried ice axe belay. Attach the rope to the shaft via a clove hitch knot.

10. A trench and slot is prepared similar to that needed for a deadman belay. The axe is pushed down into the trench, horizontally across the slope.

as to prevent the sling from rolling off. With hard ice it may not be feasible to expend the time and energy for such a bollard; *ice screws* can be used to provide a belay instead. Snow bollards are more readily prepared, and should be larger than ice bollards, at least a metre in diameter. It will probably be necessary to connect two long slings together for a snow bollard. A belay step or small ledge should be prepared about 2m below the bollard.

The design of *ice screws* has improved much since the early, 'corkscrew' type. They fall into two basic models; a thinner drive in, screw out type, and a thicker, tubular model, which may be screw in or drive in, as in the very latest design. As might be expected, the thicker type generally provides the stronger belay. One advantage of the drive-in models is their speed of placement, making them particularly useful for runners.

Belay

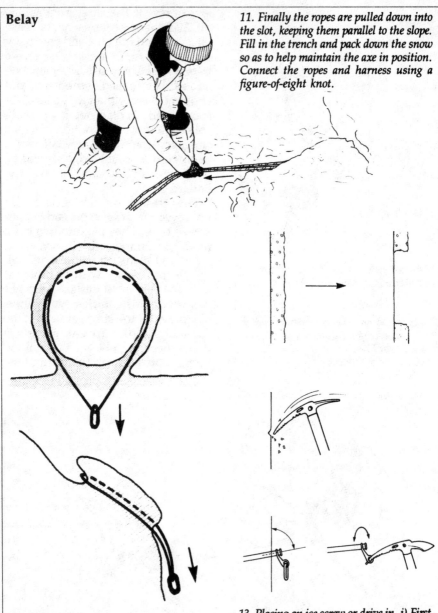

11. Finally the ropes are pulled down into the slot, keeping them parallel to the slope. Fill in the trench and pack down the snow so as to help maintain the axe in position. Connect the ropes and harness using a figure-of-eight knot.

12. To prepare a snow bollard, cut a low 'mushroom' of snow, about 50 cm in diameter, with a narrow trench all round and shaped on the uphill side so as to prevent a sling or rope from rolling up. In soft snow increase the diameter to about a metre, while with ice it may be reduced to about 30-40 cm.

13. Placing an ice screw or drive in. i) First remove any loose surface material. ii) If necessary tap a small starting hole with a pick. iii) Gently tap the screw in, at an angle of eighty degrees to the uphill slope, before hammering or screwing home and attaching a karabiner. iv) Use a pick as a ratchet for extra leverage for inserting or removing a screw.

They can also be placed in frozen turf. Whether inserting or removing screws, the ice axe provides a sensible tool for turning the screw, by inserting the pick into the eye of the screw. Begin insertion of a tubular screw by tapping a small starting hole in the selected spot then tapping the screw in some way with the hammer axe before turning. It should be placed at an angle to the slope so as to be perpendicular to the estimated direction of pull in a fall, usually meaning it will be inclined upwards by about 80 degrees. If the screw does not insert fully, tie it off with a sling using a *clove hitch*. Use two screws in preference to one, with a reasonable separation so as not to weaken the structure of the ice. Hard snow is less affected by this.

The third, effective winter belay is the *deadman*, an aluminium plate with an attached wire. The reinforced top helps prevent the relatively soft aluminium from distorting under hammer blows. The deadman, and its smaller companion the deadboy, are a development from the plywood anchors first used in the Antarctic to attach dog teams, the rectangle of wood being buried under the snow. The holding power of a properly-placed deadman in firm snow is very high indeed, and the introduction of deadmen has made the more inadequate ice axe belay unnecessary. The deadman requires at least 30cm of snow depth.

A trench is cut across the slope; about 45cm long and as narrow as possible. Next, using the axe pick, cut a slot for the deadman cable at right-angles to the first trench, this second slot will obviously be running down the slope towards the belay ledge. The deadman is then hammered into the first trench, at an angle of about 40° to the uphill slope. Meanwhile pull the cable down so that it bites further into the snow, and pulling with the cable on the slope, check that the deadman will dig down under a loading and not pop out. It may not make much difference, but peace of mind is ensured by a final packing in of extra snow on top of the trench before tying onto the karabiner on the end of the cable.

If for some reason no other belay is possible, an ice axe may be buried in a similar fashion to a deadman, with a sling tied onto the metal shaft using a clove hitch. Finally, and only as a hasty last resort, an axe may be hammered into hard snow, at an angle of about 80° to the uphill slope. Use a long sling attached to the top of the axe shaft and belay well below the axe, so that the sling runs along the surface of the snow. When wooden-shafted axes were used in such a way they often snapped, at least indicating that they were bearing a load before being pulled out. Be under no illusions, however, that the axe belay is a good system. With ingenuity, a better belay is almost always there to be found.

Belay plate. Designed by Fritz Sticht, and still referred to as the Sticht plate, this simple disk of aluminium with two slots ranks with the *deadman* as the biggest contribution to safe winter climbing in recent decades. Used in conjunction with a good belay, it enables a weak second to hold a leader fall, as friction and not physical strength does the holding. The plate can be used with single or double ropes; normally one slot is slightly thicker, to be used with an 11mm rope on its own. A *screw gate karabiner* and a short length of 4mm accessory cord completes the belay system.

The first model Sticht plate had an attached spring which held the plate away from the screwgate karabiner

Belay plate

1. Paying out the climbing ropes using a belay plate, in this case a DMM model. The right hand is holding the live ropes, which run to the other climber. The left hand is the controlling hand. The hands do not let go of the ropes but allow them to slide through when paying out or taking in. The belay plate is a few centimetres away from the screwgate karabiner, but is prevented from going further by a short loop of cord.

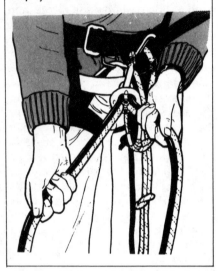

until loaded. This often caused rope jams however, and is probably unnecessary. The accessory cord goes through a small hole in the plate and is formed as a loop; it prevents the plate from sliding away from the belayer down the rope. When tied into the plate, the loop will be about 10–15cm long and will be clipped into the same karabiner as the bight of rope. The DMM Bettabrake is another contemporary model.

Chouinard has brought out the micro belay plate, an incredibly tiny version of the classic twin-slot plate, and definitely not for abseiling, as it will be unable to dissipate heat and could burn through an abseil rope. The micro belay plate weighs in at

18.5g. There are several other designs of belay devices, with the latest, the Jeff Lowe-designed Latok Tuber, incorporating a cone-shaped piece.

In using a belay plate, a bight of rope is passed through one of the slots (with two ropes, both slots are used, one for each rope). The bight is then clipped into a screwgate karabiner attached to the belayer's harness system, tied into the main rope attached to the harness. Both of the belayer's hands will hold the rope, with the hand holding the non-live rope being the controlling hand. (The live rope runs to the climbing partner.) The controlling hand should never be allowed to leave the rope, being slid along the rope when tak-

Belay plate

2. Belay plate in the locked position. The controlling hand (in this example it is the left hand) is brought up and away from the live ropes. The plate is jammed up against the screwgate karabiner, thus effectively preventing any further rope movement.

Belay plate

3. A Lowe-designed Latok Tuber in use. This hollow, truncated cone is another effective belay device. Topologically it is identical to the belay plate.

ing in or paying out. Should a fall occur or be imminent, the controlling hand brings the rope away from the live rope, increasing the angle between the two ropes and increasing the friction at the plate. The plate, under load, will be dragged up to the karabiner, effectively locking off the rope against any further movement. When belaying, think where the rope will be running, and insert the bight of rope accordingly. Another use for the belay plate is in *abseils*, particularly when using a wet or icy rope. A figure-of-eight in such circumstances may not offer sufficient friction, whereas a plate will. Better a slow abseil than your last abseil.

Benightment. See *bivouac*.

Bergschrund. Also known as a rimaye in France. Strictly speaking, this is a crevasse formed where a glacier breaks away from steeper, higher snow slopes. Also formed where a snow slope abuts against a rock wall, eg, at the foot of a rock wall. May make access to the rocks

difficult, as a deep gap can be formed which has to be crossed.

Birds. On low-lying British cliffs, and particularly on sea cliffs, climbers will have to live in agreement with the nesting season, avoiding such cliffs in spring and early summer. Birds can also be a hazard, with certain sea-birds being capable of mounting attacks on what they regard as trespassers.

Bivouac. An overnight stay in the open, either deliberate or unplanned. In the Alps, bivouacs are often planned so as to provide an early start to a route, or on a route which takes more than one day. They are often made to avoid staying in a hut. It may be necessary to bivouac, or bivvy, on the descent following a long Alpine route. Unplanned bivouacs, or benightments, can happen due to sudden deterioration of the weather, too late a start, unexpected difficulties, too slow a pace on the route, or any combination of these. A well-planned bivouac in a good spot can be a delight. A benightment can be hell, even if equipped.

Bivvy gear in the Alps is a compromise between weight and comfort. The minimum for comfort will normally include: closed cell *camping mat* (need not be full-length, half-length might suffice), *stove*, small pot for heating water, soup etc, sleeping bag, and a bivvy bag, which may range from a basic, strong poly bag to a luxurious Gore-tex version. Some climbers prefer a *duvet jacket* to a sleeping bag; in winter both might be needed.

A bivouac site should be chosen with safety in mind and comfort under body. In the Alps especially, avoid spots which may be struck by lightning such as summits and ridges. These would be exposed to wind in any case. If forced to use a narrow, exposed spot, tie on and ensure that all equipment is secured. Better to collect water before settling in for the night, as it may be frozen in the morning. Take a warm *water bottle* into your sleeping bag so as to prevent it from freezing overnight and to provide an element of heating. If still wearing leather boots bring them into the sleeping bag too: with double nylon boots, which will not freeze solid overnight, the inners can be kept on for warmth in the morning. In winter, a planned bivvy may utilize a *snow hole*. This may require some forward planning and several hours' hard work to build.

An unplanned bivvy, or benightment, particularly in a Scottish winter, is not recommended. Even if emergency gear is carried, as it should be, it will be a long, cold, and uncomfortable night (very few climbers carry the weight of a sleeping bag, only some a Gore-tex bag, though all should have at least a strong poly bag). Strongly consider climbing on by headtorch, if conditions and fitness allow. If resigned to a night out attempt to find shelter from the wind, which otherwise is a very effective heat remover. Spare clothing, eg, an extra sweater, will help. Many *rucksacks* have a length of closed cell mat running down their back; this will help insulate a cold seat.

Bollards. Snow or ice belays cut out from the slope. See *belay*.

Bolts. Metal expansion bolts inserted into a pre-drilled hole in an otherwise blank face of rock. Bolts can be used for a *belay*, *runner*, or as an *aid point*. Their use, particularly in the UK, is controversial, and often unpopular.

Boots. Climbing footwear, specialized

Boots

1. *A traditional, double, leather mountaineering boot — the Guida Walker. These will take any crampons, including rigids and step-ins, as they are stiff boots with an integral steel plate in the sole and deep welts for bindings. Vibram sole and heel.*

2. *The modern double mountaineering boot — in this case the Koflach Ultra. The ankle section is hinged, to allow more comfortable flexing (and prevent the boot ankle from suffering cracking). Deep welts front and rear take step-in crampon bindings. A slight up-curve of the sole — known as a rocker — makes for easier walking. A small insert (usually of Sorbothane) in the heel gives some degree of cushioning. Vibram sole and heel.*

towards walking, rock climbing, or winter use. Walking boots cover a wide spectrum of preferences, from cheap trainers to expensive leather boots providing a degree of ankle support. The most effective sole is still probably a rubber moulded into the Vibram pattern. This was an Italian invention, dating from 1935, and named after its developer, *Vitali Bram*ini. It became widespread following the Second World War. Over the last decade other patterns and types of rubber have been introduced, particularly for lighter weight walking boots. Though more comfortable, the grip on wet rock and muddy ground is definitely inferior. These new boots also have a cutaway heel. This may make it slightly less jarring when setting down the foot on a hard path, but on descent there is no edge to grip the substrate. Leather boots require basic maintenance to prolong their life. Clean off mud etc after use, allow to dry over several days without heating. Every now and again apply your favourite proofing, rubbing it into the seams especially. Resole boots before the uppers become damaged. Some local shoe repairers can do Vibram soles; if in difficulty most climbing shops have a service for this.

For rock climbing a smooth, high-friction rubber sole is used in conjunction with a lightweight, thin upper. Rock boots have recently begun to develop towards a higher-friction but softer rubber sole, and, in some models, an upper which has almost disappeared. The only criterion for a rock boot used to be a sole with a lateral rigidity for *edging*, and flexibility lengthwise so that slabs could be climbed.

With ever-steeper rock being climbed with ever-fewer holds, the rock boot has further evolved along two lines: smearing, or edging. The smearing boot has a softer and stickier sole, with a less hard edge. It is for climbing lacking good footholds, where the feet are using sole friction to maintain purchase. The upper in a smearing boot is minimal. Pointed toes can help obtain a foothold in toe pockets. The fit is normally painfully tight for high standard climbing.

An edging boot is closer to older models in that a harder, sharper edge to the sole allows small wrinkles and better holds on the rock to be used as positive holds. With use they will blur and soften at the edges. Boot design is developing so fast however, that these distinctions may not be so clear in the near future. Talk to active climbers, try on different boots, ask yourself what type of climbing you will be concentrating on, what rock types you will be climbing on. And speak to a friendly bank manager.

Winter boots have the requirement

Boots

3. *A slightly lighter, single mountaineering boot, the Scarpa Fitzroy. Leather upper, rubber rand, Vibram sole and heel. This boot is sufficiently stiff to take a hinged crampon, but has more flex to allow for less traumatic walking.*

4. *Specialized rock boot, the Scarpa Rockmaster. The heel is low-cut, while the rubber is high-friction.*

of fairly rigid soles so as to allow the use of *crampons,* good ankle support, and a reasonably high and water-proof ankle cuff. The use of nylon and plastic shells has been a recent innovation, providing boots which are both lighter and (for most users) more comfortable than traditional leather boots. The expected reduction in price, naturally, did not occur. Most winter boots made from synthetic materials are double, with a soft leather or synthetic removable inner boot used in conjunction with a hard shell soled in the Vibram pattern. The spread of *step-in bindings* for crampons has seen winter boots made with projecting welts at toes and heels, similar to ski boots. Winter boots are often worn with *gaiters,* though sadly there still seems to be little cooperation between boot and gaiter manufacturers.

Bothies. An old cottage or house used in a casual fashion by walkers and climbers. There are many such bothies, especially in Scotland, open to all. Many are maintained by volunteers, the members of the Mountain Bothies Association (MBA) being prominent.

Bouldering. A form of training for some climbers, an end in itself to others. In its most widely-accepted sense this is the free climbing of isolated, small rock features, most often rock boulders of up to about 10m in height. Normally no equipment is used other than rock boots and *chalk.* Climbing *ethics* are strongly evident

---

Bowline

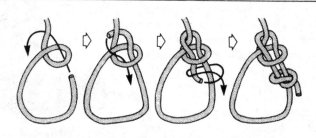

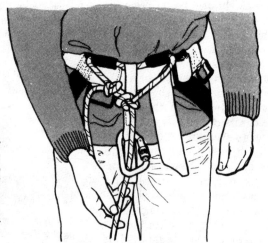

This shows a bowline knot, used to tie into a Whillans Sit Harness, to which it is also connected via a screwgate karabiner. The bowline knot is finished off with a stopper knot.

Braking

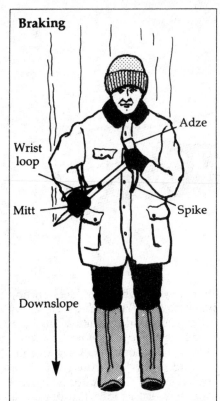

Adze

Wrist loop

Mitt

Spike

Downslope

1. The ice axe braking position, viewed from the slope. The pick is in use here, with much of the body weight hunched over the axe head (held in left hand in this example). Keep the feet off the slope preferably, unless in soft snow, when they can also be used for braking.

in bouldering, with routes consisting of accepted combinations of holds and no use of extra holds from neighbouring routes. Some boulder problems, as the routes are called, may take years of effort before fitness, experience and determined effort succeed. Along the way, fitness, experience and determination have been added to a climber's ammunition!

Bowline. A knot commonly used for attaching the main climbing rope to the harness. It has the advantages of being easy to tie and adjust, but should be finished with a thumb knot or *stopper* as security against working loose. It can be tied through a harness or, in an emergency or where no harness is used (eg, to protect a scrambling move on an otherwise easy ridge walk), it can be tied round the waist.

Braking with ice axe. Also called self-arrest, this technique of halting an accidental slip on a snow slope can save your life. It must be practised so as to become automatic, as one can accelerate at an alarming rate on even an easy slope. Find a safe snow slope, one which has no projecting or hidden boulders and one whose angle flattens out to give a safe runout should initial practice runs fail! The intention, should a slip or fall happen, is to end up in the basic braking position as quickly as possible, and certainly within a second or two of the start of the slide. To take much longer means building up speed and kinetic energy, which could make it impossible to hold the axe when braking commences.

The basic braking position is face towards the slope, head upwards, with the axe held firmly down and across the trunk, one hand on top of the axe at join of adze and pick (fingers on top, thumb below), the other on the shaft just above the spike. The pick is normally going to do the actual braking, though in very wet snow the adze may have to be used for effective braking. For most people out walking, holding the axe by the head, shaft dangling down, so that the pick points backwards, allows the axe to be easily brought into the braking position. The axe head will be close to the shoulder in the braking position.

First practise sliding down in a sitting position then rolling over to face

Braking

2. *View from the side showing braking position (axe head in right hand in this example).*

the snow, simultaneously allowing the axe pick to score into the snow. Too fast or deep with the pick and it may be dragged out of your grasp. Once it is biting increase the depth of the pick. Try and keep the boots off the snow surface, as on hard snow they can catch. For this reason, initial practice should be without crampons. Only when confident should you try braking wearing crampons (*'Beware the Jabberwock, my son! The jaws that bite, the claws that catch!'*). A fall in a feet-first position should not be too difficult to control. Next try a head-first fall. Rotate into a feet-first fall by using the axe like a rudder, stretching it to one side and gently braking so as to swing the body round. Then brake to halt as usual. The most difficult fall, except perhaps a confusing, tumbling descent, will be a head-first, face-up one. Practice all of these until wet but happy in the knowledge that a fall can be stopped. Thirty minutes' practice when starting out in winter can safeguard years of climbing and walking. **Tip**. Refresher practices every few years make sense.

Breeches. Climbing trousers ending just below the knees and cut loosely for comfort and flexibility. They can be opened below the knee for ventilation. Seats and knees are usually reinforced. Modern materials include stretch synthetics, comfortable, light and snow-resistant. Traditionalists still use tweed, which blends in with the surroundings and when frozen provides useful sticking powers in winter.

Bridging. Technique used to climb wide chimneys, or walls on widely-spaced footholds. In a chimney, left hand and foot will be on one wall, and right hand and foot on the other, the spacing possible limited by the length and flexibility of the climber's limbs and joints. A corner can be bridged, feet using friction holds only. Bridging can be less strenuous a way of progress than alternatives, as much of the work can be done by the larger leg muscles.

Brocken spectre. Named after an optical phenomenon commonly seen in the Brocken Mountains of Germany. When a climber is at about cloud level with a low angle of sunlight behind, the climber's shadow may be thrown onto a backdrop of cloud, somewhat enlarged. There will often be an associated coloured halo, called a glory, seen round the shadow's head.

Buttress. A defined mass of rock protruding from the side of a mountain. It may have flanking gullies or chimneys, and if long and narrow may be termed a *ridge*.

Cagoule. Form of hooded nylon *anorak* becoming less common. From

the French for a monk's habit. Reaching to the knee, with no front zip.

Cairn. Pile of rocks built by climbers and/or walkers, usually on summits but occasionally elsewhere, as a rough guide to walkers.

Calls while climbing. To prevent confusion between roped climbers, a system of shouted messages has been arrived at over the years. When the leader has gained a belay ledge and is securely tied on, the call is 'Belayed!', or 'Tied on!'. This alerts the second, who, if the position is safe, can begin dismantling the belay. The leader then shouts 'Taking in!', as the

Bridging

1. In this steep corner, the climber is using his left foot on the wall to help keep him in balance. The right foot is also bridged out, opposing the forces pushing him out and off.

Bridging

2. Here a wide chimney is bridged, using footholds on the edges. The left hand is pushing down on a flat hold.

rope is pulled up. When all the spare rope has been pulled up, the second informs the leader by shouting 'That's me!'. The leader will now check that all is ready, the belay is prepared, and that the ropes are correctly installed through the *belay plate* before shouting 'Climb when you're ready!'. With a final shout of 'Climbing!', the second can begin. A rope who climb together regularly will obviously modify these shouts slightly, but the essence remains. Two other calls are important, and must not be confused. These are 'Slack!', when a second requires more rope to be released by the belayer, and 'Take in!', when a second requires more rope to be pulled up by the belayer. 'Take in!' can be quickly and effortlessly transformed into 'Tight rope!', when a second is in trouble. A common beginner's mistake is often to shout 'Take in

Camming devices

1. A Flexible Friend in a horizontal crack, used with an extender and karabiner.

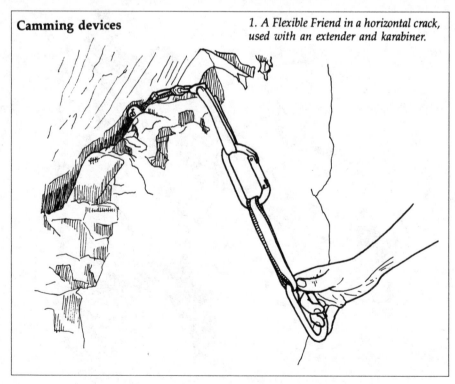

slack!'. When communication is poor, due to wind or being out of sight, this can obviously lead to a misunderstanding! An important warning call is 'Below!', when rock or ice is falling or is dislodged accidentally.

Camming devices. Mechanical protection devices designed to jam in cracks over a range of diameters. Perhaps best known in the UK are the series of *Friends* manufactured by Wild Country, a spring-loaded set of four curved, opposing aluminium alloy cams, allowing fixation in parallel-sided or even flared cracks. These were developed by Ray Jardine and Greg Lowe in the 1970s, American climbers used to parallel-sided and flared cracks difficult to protect. Other makes include the Metiolus 3-Cam, the HB, the Wild Country Micromate (a tri-cam device, as opposed to the four-cammed Friends), the DMM Rollers, and the Chouinard Camalot (magical pun?). A camming device in a good position will jam even more firmly under load. Though perhaps not quite as secure as more traditional *chockstones*, camming devices have made possible protection where otherwise none might have been found. There are several camming devices which do not incorporate springs, described under chockstones.

The positioning of a standard Friend has to be thought out carefully, with the stem pointing, where possible, towards the probable direction of pull during a fall. This will normally be down and slightly out, making sure that the two triggers are accessible. Also avoid using close to the extreme range of travel of the cams, best to place with the cams about halfway closed. They can often be placed quickly, but also are prone to work their own way deeper into a crack, when they can be impossible

to remove. Carry a *nut key* which has a double hook on the end for removing awkward customers, such as the DMM model. The intelligent placement of such devices is basically the same as for chockstones in general. If a Friend is fitted into a shallow or horizontal crack, so that much of its stem is projecting out, then it should be tied off. A loop of 4mm accessory cord through the first hole above the triggers (ie, towards the cams) will do the trick.

The latest design of camming device from Wild Country, the Flexible Friend, has a flexible steel cable stem, making it less likely to be swivelled by rope movement, or, for that matter, less likely to 'walk' its way into or out of a crack. Sizes 0, 0.5, 1, and 1.5 have a strength of between 1200 and 1400kg. The expansion range of a number 1, for example, is from 19 to 29mm, though you should not use it at either end of this range. The number 1 weighs in at 74g. The standard Friends come in half sizes, from 1 to 4, with strengths of 1400kg.

The DMM Rollers, sized from A to E and with colour-coded plastic sleeves over their twin wired stems, are also flexible, with an unusual design featuring a small, barbell-shaped device 'rolling' over a wedge, thereby giving a range of jamming sizes. The Roller also has the disconcerting habit of nipping fingers between the trigger handle and the plastic sleeve, though no doubt this will soon be rectified. They work well in pockets, perhaps suiting them to limestone routes.

The smoothest actioned camming device is the Chouinard Camalot, or Spring Loaded Camming Device (SLCD) as the American climber and manufacturer Yvon Chouinard would have it. In four sizes, 1 to 4, this device has a double axle and a

Camming devices

2. A Flexible Friend used as a runner, with an extender.

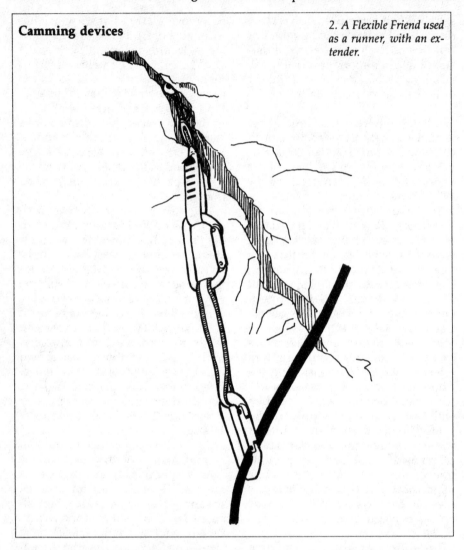

flexible cable handle. Each individual Camalot will fit a larger range of crack sizes than its rivals, while it can even be used as a normal chockstone in its fully open or 'umbrella' configuration, as both axles support the open cams. The flexible handle, like the Flexible Friend, allows the Camalot to be used in horizontal placements with minimal risk of stem breakage. Another well-designed plus is the ability to withdraw the Camalot using one finger on the loop handle.

Strengths of 1100kg are quoted, and the Camalot, like all Chouinard hardware, is tested to half its quoted strength before leaving the factory.

Camping. Climbing is often pleasantly and conveniently combined with carrying and living in a tent. Many mountain holidays or weekends are difficult to arrange otherwise. Lightweight tents, made of nylon, have made the load much lighter, though cooking utensils and

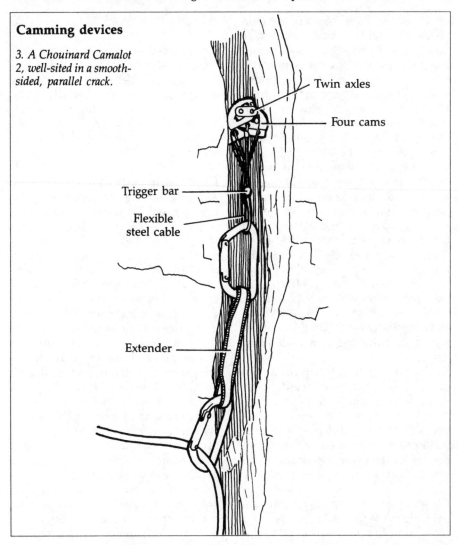

Camming devices

3. A Chouinard Camalot 2, well-sited in a smooth-sided, parallel crack.

Twin axles

Four cams

Trigger bar

Flexible steel cable

Extender

sleeping bags will still have to be carried. During Himalayan *expeditions*, tents are often used at convenient sites on the peak, though for most other climbing the tent is used as a base from which to attempt a route.

Camping mats. Rectangular closed cell foam mat, light to carry, especially if less than body length. Does not absorb water and provides excellent insulation from rough, cold ground during a *bivouac* or while

camping. Many rucksacks have short lengths built into their back, useful during an involuntary bivouac, but for a pre-planned bivouac or camping trip a longer mat is preferable.

Chalk. a) Athlete's chalk in powder form, magnesium carbonate, used to provide drier hands and better friction in rock climbing. Should be used for the harder grades only, though occasionally the tell-tale white blotches on the rock have been seen

on classic V. Diffs. Kept in a nylon chalk bag with a draw cord top, attached to the climbing *harness* and hung at the back for a convenient dip into when needed. Also provides psychological help for many a hard move. **Tip**. When climbing in a high wind a few small stones in the bag may prevent it from being blown upside down and enveloping you in a cosmic cloud of chalk! It is possible, in some of the more enlightened retailers, to buy 'ecological' chalk, coloured in muted browns, greens or greys, so as to be less obtrusive on the rock. It costs about 25% more than the white variety, which seems a small price to pay for a tidier crag, though it is not quite as effective as the white variety. Also available are small chalk bags, called 'digit dippers', designed for climbing walls where only the finger tips will be in use!
b) The soft chalk cliffs on the south coast of England have recently provided some enthusiastic winter climbers with a substitute venue, climbing with *front pointing* gear just as in winter. Very steep and hard climbing, one major disadvantage seems to be instability on a large scale.

Cheating. Mountaineering is unusual in being (so far) a fairly unregulated sport. It is, in other words, up to the individual climber to monitor ethics, and stay, if possible, within the unwritten but generally accepted rules of the game. To use aid on an easy route is unethical, for example, unless there is an emergency. To use fixed ropes and multi-day siege tactics on a British route is similarly cheating, though until recently it was acceptable in the Himalaya. Difficulties of definition arise at the edges of the sport, eg, at the very highest grades. Basically speaking, however, a climber will usually know when

cheating is in progress.

Chimney. **a)** A steep break in a rock face, often with two parallel walls, like the gap between two closely adjoining buildings. Usually wide enough to admit a climber though still permitting the walls to be used for *backing up* or *bridging*. **b)** To climb a *chimney*.

Chockstones. Also known as nuts. The original, natural chockstone is a stone or rock jammed in a crack, permitting protection or a belay using a sling or threaded rope. These can be useful, though they are obviously only sporadically present, and beginning some time in the 1960s artificial chockstones were made from standard engineering nuts, the threads being drilled out to prevent wear of the sling. They are now conveniently manufactured from aluminium alloys, with drilled holes for sling or wire to be inserted. Nuts come in all shapes and sizes, from very small wedges made of brass with swaged wire known as *micros*, to considerably larger *hexentrics*. There remain two basic shapes however, the wedge, and the hexentric.
The wedge may have classically flat faces, or have gently curved surfaces, which work more efficiently in cracks. The smaller wedges will be bought mounted permanently on wire for greater strength, but many climbers normally select their own length of 7mm or 8mm accessory cord, or 5.5mm *Kevlar*, and finish the nut themselves. The best design of wedges is epitomized by Chouinard Stoppers and Wild Country Rocks. Cassin also has a similar range, called the Halfmoons, recognized by their colour-coded, anodized finish. In all of these chockstones, the two narrow sides are flat, tapering from top to bottom, while the two wide faces are

curved, one convex, the other concave. This design gives a camming action in a crack.

Stoppers are sized from 1 through 13. The first three are straight-sided. All are obtainable fitted with *swaged*, galvanized steel cable, while sizes 10 through 13 are available loose, with holes drilled ready to accept 5.5mm *Kevlar* cord. Sizes six and upwards have strengths of 1100kg. Corners of Stoppers are slightly rounded, making them easier to remove. Wild Country Rocks are available on wire, sizes 1 through 9, and also pre-fitted with stitched tape. Their finish is similar to the Stoppers, with a slightly less shiny surface and the same rounded corners.

An interesting recent development from DMM is the range of chockstones called Walnuts. These are shaped like Stoppers and Rocks, with the additional feature of a shallow scoop on each of the wide faces. These, like the Campbell saddle-wedge chockstones, allow the placements to be even more secure if the chockstones are fitted snugly round small irregularities on the wall of a crack. Walnuts are available in sizes 1 through 9 on wire, plus 9 on *Kevlar* cord, giving the latter a quoted strength of 1500kg.

The hexentric chockstone is a refinement of a basic hexagon or six-sided shape, in that the faces are not all of the same size, thereby allowing more configurations and a better chance of successful jamming in a crack. See *protection*. The hexentric is basically a hexagonal tube, which makes it very light for its size and strength. In sizes 1 through 11, the first three can be had wired, with a strength of 1100kg. Sizes 4 upwards have a strength of 1100kg, when fitted with 8mm rope. When fitted with the newer *Kevlar* 5.5mm rope they have a strength of 1400kg. This means that the holes drilled in the hexes and stoppers for rope are now too large. Thread the *Kevlar* through clear plastic tubing, which is also inserted into these holes, and a neat finish will be obtained. Why clear? You want to be able to check on the conditions of all ropes and slings regularly, including chockstone ropes.

Micro-wires take the shape, commonly, of a straight-sided wedge. They allow shallow grooves and poorly defined cracks to be used where Rocks or Stoppers would be too large. Brass has been used for these small nuts, with steel cable silver-soldered into the heads. Testing has indicated however that the nuts can fail, not because of the cable, but due to the brass deforming and shearing out of cracks. This has led Chouinard at least to use steel for the heads as well, finding them on test to be as strong as the cable. Other micro-wires include RPs, designed by the Australian climber Roland Pauligk and sized from 0 through 5 on wire, and HBs, designed by Hugh Banner, which have a transverse asymmetric taper.

The smallest sizes of any micro are for marginal placements, when nothing better can be found. The strength of a size 0 RP, for example, is a lowly 360kg. In most cases, however, the rock will probably let you down before the chockstone does, making it even more crucial to place these nuts with great care.

There are any number of other designs of chockstones, some good, some not so good, and some, to be perfectly honest, quite bizarre. Consumer testing very quickly sorts out the good from the poor however, while the bizarre can be found collecting dust on any retailer's gear rack. Plastic nuts have been tried, multiple-sized, stacking nuts, giant T-

Clove hitch
(see page 47)

A knot used for belaying.
i) Form two loops as shown.
ii) Then slide one loop behind the other.

shaped nuts, swivel-headed pentagonal nuts etc, etc. Many can be found cheaply, as can the older models of chockstones, usually straight-sided wedges, symmetrical hexagons and so on. They do work, but much less efficiently than modern designs, and they cannot be recommended as purchases. Wait a little longer, save up, and buy the best — it's your neck on the rock.

Classic. An occasionally over-used word, usually applied to a route which has become recognized as being of very high quality. Also used in connection with outdated techniques, eg, the classic method of abseiling.

Clothing. The basic clothing required for hill walking includes a good waterproof *anorak*, a pair of warm *breeches*, long woollen socks, long-sleeved shirt and warm sweater. Add a woollen hat or *balaclava*, mitts, and overtrousers or overbreeches, and we have the basic set of clothing. For walking in winter warm underwear is usually worn and a pair of gaiters added to the outfit. The above clothing will also suffice for winter climbing, with perhaps the sweater being upgraded. A cotton ski poloneck worn under the main shirt is remarkably efficient at preventing snow going down one's neck, but most climbers do not seem to have discovered this convenience yet (use the type with zip necks, giving ventilation while approaching the climb). On a warm day shorts may be worn, but unless the outing is a very short one remaining close to base then breeches should also be carried.

For rock climbing the emphasis is on clothing which is fairly close-fitting and yet allows easy movement. Stretch tracksuit trousers are ideal. For the harder climber who

Coiling rope — standard method

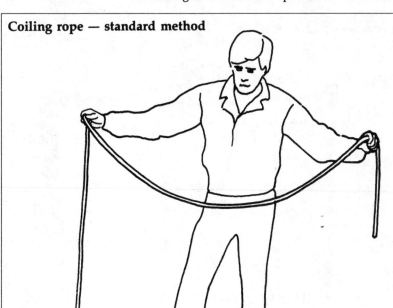

1. Hold one end in (left) hand, and with about 20 cm to spare, swing both hands out to side.

2. Building up loops in left hand.

Coiling rope — standard method

3. *And more loops!*

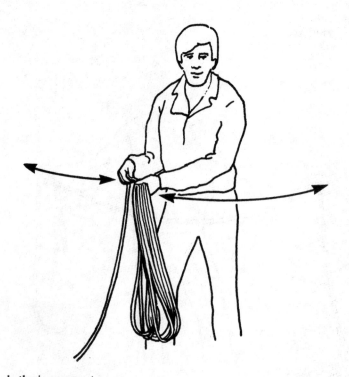

4. *A rhythmic movement helps minimize tiredness.*

Coiling rope — standard method

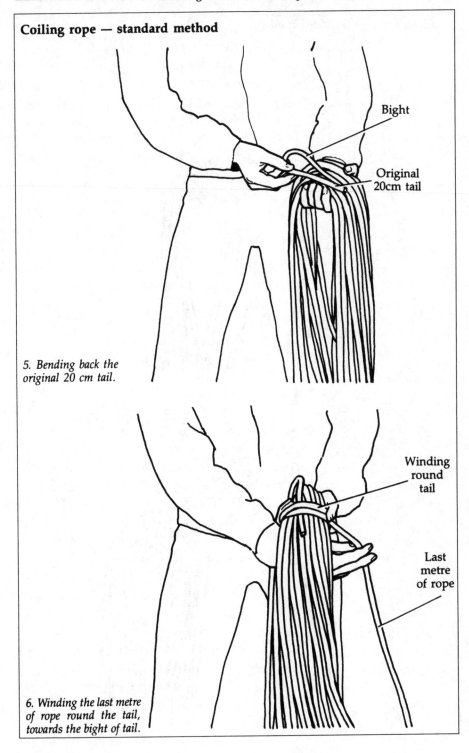

Bight

Original
20cm tail

5. Bending back the
original 20 cm tail.

Winding
round
tail

Last
metre
of rope

6. Winding the last metre
of rope round the tail,
towards the bight of tail.

Coiling rope — standard method

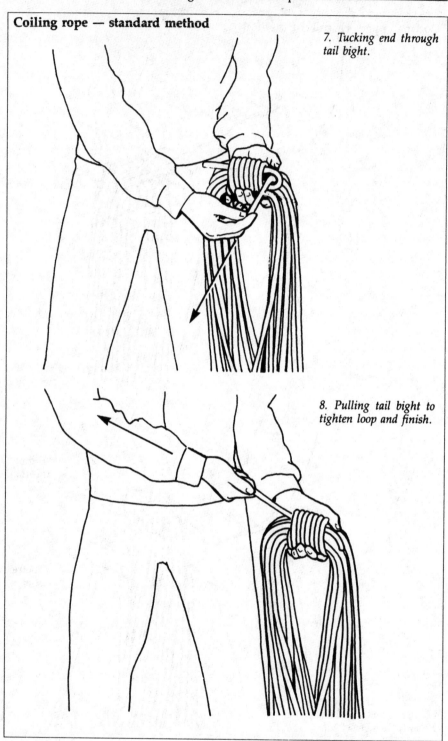

7. Tucking end through tail bight.

8. Pulling tail bight to tighten loop and finish.

must draw attention, there is a range of very bright tights. The penalty of failure while wearing the latter is ridicule and, worse, being ignored. Things can become awkward when rock climbing on a cooler mountain cliff. A relatively windproof, zip-fronted *pile fabric* sweater may work well on a cool day, as long as it is fairly lightweight. The longer *anorak* used for walking or winter climbing is too cumbersome for rock climbing, but then rainy conditions are not normally chosen deliberately for rock climbing.

Clove hitch. A simple, fast knot, used for attaching the main climbing rope to belays or tying off pegs or ice screws. It has a slightly lower strength than the *figure-of-eight* knot however, which it should not replace as the main belay knot (60% versus 62% strength). The clove hitch is useful for situations where speed is of the essence, eg, tying off a third man, fast belaying in the Alps. (See drawing, page 42.)

Coiling rope. One could simply stuff the climbing rope into the rucksack after a route, but this takes up more space and the ends tend to become lost. The human mind likes regularity and order, so we coil the rope. It is also probably easier to pay out the rope from a neat pile of coils. Assuming right-handedness, hold one end in the left hand, with about 20cm left spare. Swing both hands out to the sides, allowing rope to slide through the right hand, then bring hands together and transfer the point on the rope held by the right hand to the left (which will now obviously be holding two points and one coil). Repeat this movement, each time adding to the coils held by the left hand. A rhythmic movement helps minimize tiredness, especially after a good day's climbing. Stop when about a metre of rope is left, bend back the original 20cm tail above the top of the coils and using the last metre of rope bind this tail to the coils, winding towards the bight of the tail. Finally tuck the end through the tail bight and pull the tail so as to tighten the loop and secure the rope. A well-made rope should not kink too much on coiling. If it does, it may need to be straightened out by uncoiling to its full length on a grass field. Ropes will often form into a figure-of-eight shape when coiled, this is due to their construction and it is better to put up with this minor inconvenience.

There have been unfortunate deaths to climbers moving on steep ground carrying a coiled rope, due to the coils slipping at an awkward moment. To coil a rope when there remains scrambling to be done and the rope must be carried securely without a sack, start from the middle of the rope. A small piece of coloured tape or a mark with dye at this point on the rope can save time, otherwise start from the ends, pulling through both ends to find the middle point. Begin coiling with the middle in the left hand and coil the rope double until about 2–3m is left. Begin binding this tail round the top part of the coils, make several such turns, insert a bight of the tail through the main coils and tuck the tail through the bight. The rope can then be slung behind one's back with an end brought over each shoulder, passed underarm, behind the rope, securing it onto one's body, then tied in front with a *reef knot*.

Coire. Gaelic for the feature found in glaciated mountains, a scooped-out hollow usually backed by a ridge or plateau and often containing a small lochan.

Coiling rope for scrambling

1. Find the middle point of rope and begin coiling as in the standard method.

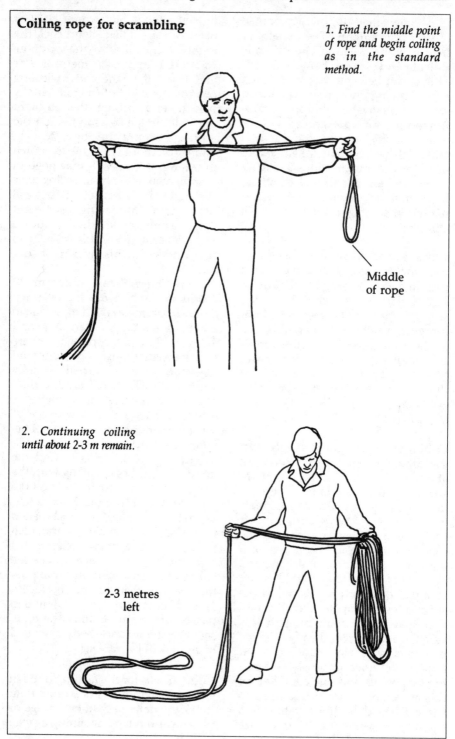

Middle
of rope

2. Continuing coiling until about 2-3 m remain.

2-3 metres
left

Coiling rope for scrambling

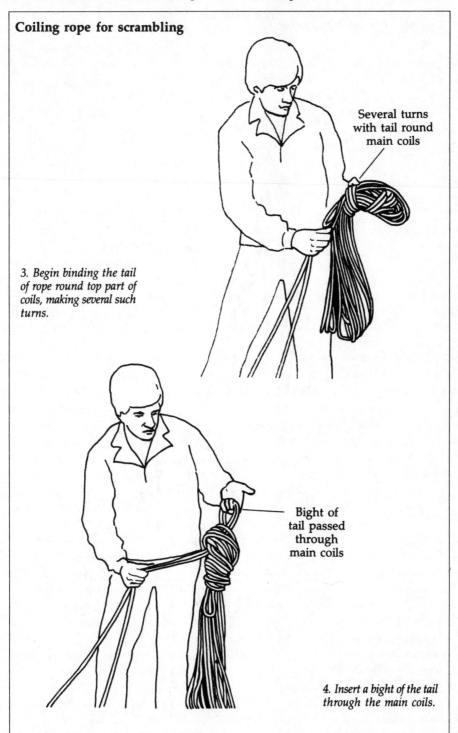

Several turns
with tail round
main coils

*3. Begin binding the tail
of rope round top part of
coils, making several such
turns.*

Bight of
tail passed
through
main coils

*4. Insert a bight of the tail
through the main coils.*

Coiling rope for scrambling

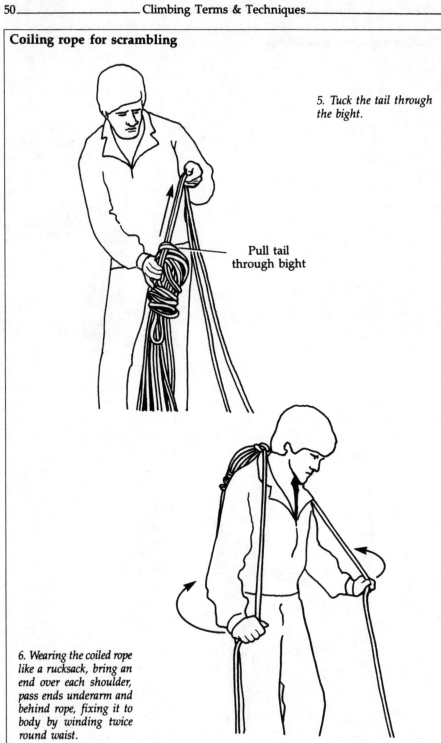

5. Tuck the tail through the bight.

Pull tail through bight

6. Wearing the coiled rope like a rucksack, bring an end over each shoulder, pass ends underarm and behind rope, fixing it to body by winding twice round waist.

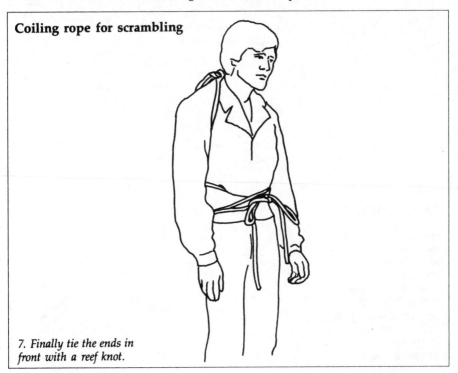

Coiling rope for scrambling

7. Finally tie the ends in front with a reef knot.

Combined tactics. An increasingly rare technique used on a route, where the leader stands on the second's shoulders in order to overcome some difficulty. Still occasionally used as a last-gasp effort in winter, perhaps in order to reach the foot of an icefall.

Committing. A move is said to be committing when it is likely to be impossible to reverse safely. Also applies to the lead of a hard pitch involving several difficult moves in sequence. Requires a bold mentality.

Communication. See *calls while climbing*.

Compass. A hand-held navigational aid for movement over the mountains which includes a pivoted magnetic needle indicating magnetic north. See *bearing*.

Corner. A rock feature, resembling the inside angle of a partly opened book. There may be a crack in the angle, allowing it to be climbed, or it may have to be climbed by *bridging*. The contrasting feature is an edge or *arête*, resembling the spine of a partly opened book. Early mountaineering writers often used corner when describing an edge, as the meaning has shifted with time.

Cornice. An overhanging curve of snow often formed by wind at the head of a *gully* or at the side of a *ridge*. These are not always obvious from above and are therefore dangerous, collapsing without warning. Collapsing cornices are a frequent cause of avalanches during a thaw. If a cornice completely blocks the exit to a gully, escape might be made by digging a tunnel through to the top. This can be dangerous, tiring, and time-consuming. Cornices vary in size from

Cornice

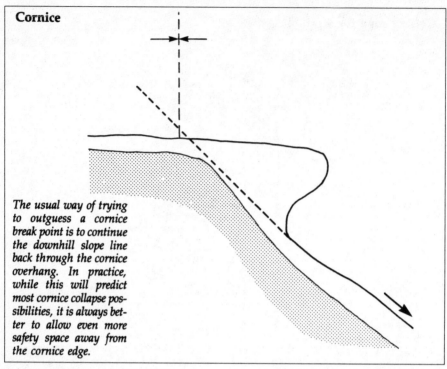

The usual way of trying to outguess a cornice break point is to continue the downhill slope line back through the cornice overhang. In practice, while this will predict most cornice collapse possibilities, it is always better to allow even more safety space away from the cornice edge.

country to country, with some monsters particularly to be found in the Americas. They share a common feature however, and that is the break line, the theoretical point at which they might part from the slope. The break line is often calculated by continuing the angle of slope over which the cornice hangs back through the cornice to the other side. When walking along the ridge containing a cornice, stay below the break line, which can be lower than theory might predict. More than one climber has been killed by belaying at the top of a gully, at a point thought to be far enough back to be off the cornice.

Couloir. French word for a *gully*, a deep chasm between rock buttresses. As this feature is usually formed by the erosion of weaker or shattered rock, there is normally an associated amount of loose debris. Couloirs are therefore usually safer and better as

winter climbs. Having said that, when warmed by the sun snow and ice will begin to fall. In the Alps couloirs form many classic routes, though many are best climbed well before, or after, the sun has loosened them. Some couloirs are dangerous at all times and should be avoided if possible. If a couloir does have to be climbed or descended, stay close to the walls if possible, as these can provide shelter and good belays. Avoid the natural fall line of the couloir, often indicated by a channel cut by falling debris. Climb on hard snow and not soft; it's both easier and safer to do so. Late in an Alpine season couloirs may contain much tough, black ice, formed by countless thaw–freeze cycles. Unless looking for hard times avoid these.

Courses. It is possible to learn the basics of climbing by going on an organized course. Advantages are that a properly run and taught course, held perhaps at one of the National Outdoor Centres, will safely teach you the rudiments and theoretically make you a safe beginner quickly. Disadvantages are that they are not cheap, and that they lack the excitement of one's own first faltering steps. A good compromise is to join a local club and learn from more experienced climbers, hopefully forming a partnership during the process. There are now many private courses, run from all sorts of bases in the mountains. Courses in hill walking, rock climbing, winter climbing, alpine climbing. Courses should not be a substitute for the personal learning experience, but if embarking on such a route then at least ensure that instructors are qualified.

Cow's tail. See *aid climbing*.

Cracks. A narrow fissure in a rock wall, perhaps allowing hands or fingers to be inserted but too narrow for one's body. A common source of holds on a rock climb, cracks come in a huge variety of shapes, sizes and usefulness. They may be horizontal, when they can provide the most useful holds, angled or vertical, when they may have to be used with a *jamming* technique. Vertical cracks can also be climbed by a *layback* technique. For *protection* and/or *belaying*, cracks may be used for *chockstones*, *pegs* or *friends*.

Crampons. A metal framework fastened to the underside of winter climbing boots with (commonly) twelve downward pointing spikes spaced out round the edge of the frame. These spikes are arranged in pairs along each crampon, with one or two pairs at the front inclined forward at an angle. The use of step-in bindings is increasing, permitting faster attachment, a great advantage during a cold start. The origin of crampons is probably agricultural use in the Austrian Tyrol, to allow haymaking on steep ground. They were developed as climbing tools, in particular by Austro-German mountaineers.

Crampons permit safe and easy movement over snow and ice where otherwise steps might have to be cut, a time-consuming business. On steep snow and ice the front points come into use, the boots being kicked into the slope. There are many models of crampons available, but if they are intended to be used for climbing routes, as opposed to walking over the lower hills in winter then two basic rules should be observed: they should be worn in conjunction with stiff boots, and they should have twelve points. Crampons with ten points can be bought, lacking the two forward inclined points. They can be used for walking, but otherwise there seems little point in doing without the extra pair of points which would allow at least easy routes to be more safely climbed.

The main decision over the purchase of a pair of crampons is whether to buy hinged (or articulated) or rigid crampons. Hinged crampons have their two sections, front and rear or sole and heel, connected via a metal bar. The crampon can be adjusted for length using this bar, though one session of adjustment per pair of boots is normally sufficient. Hinged crampons are generally more suited for *mixed climbing*, ie, routes involving rocks as well as snow and ice. Rigid crampons, including the plastic based Footfangs, are designed for steep ice, where normally the front points will be extensively used. They provide a better platform on ice and so less fatigue for overworked calf muscles on routes

Crampons

1. A pair of stiff mountain boots mounted on Salewa Hard Ice Classic model of crampon. These are hinged, giving some little flexibility for walking and buttress climbing. There are 12 points, and the straps are French style, with separate ankle and toe straps. The hinge bar allows the length of the crampon to be adjusted, permitting a small range of boot sizes to be fitted.

These Salewa adjustable, hinged crampons are perhaps the best pair of crampons ever designed for general use.

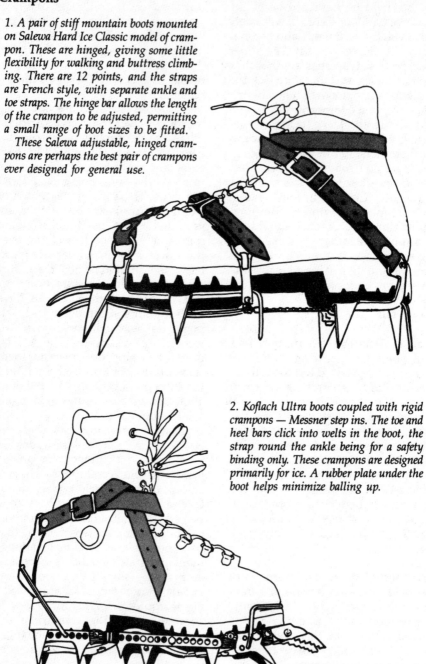

2. Koflach Ultra boots coupled with rigid crampons — Messner step ins. The toe and heel bars click into welts in the boot, the strap round the ankle being for a safety binding only. These crampons are designed primarily for ice. A rubber plate under the boot helps minimize balling up.

Crampons

Toestrap

Toe ring

Ankle strap

Anti-balling up plate

3. *Two other models of rigid crampon, fitted with straps.*
Above: Chouinard/Salewa rigids, with separate toe and heel straps. The toe strap runs through a metal ring, making this a secure strap system.
Below: Simond rigids. The long ankle strap runs through both toe and heel straps. There is a rubber anti-balling up plate.

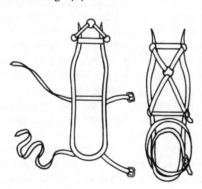

4. *Fastening a crampon strap using a toe ring. i) Right crampon shown from above. The straps are always fastened on the outside of feet, to avoid catching on holds or the other foot. ii) Run the toe strap through the ring then fasten to buckle on outside of foot. The ankle strap is wound completely round the ankle then fastened through the buckle on the outside of the foot.*

consisting mostly of snow and ice. However they have little disadvantage on mixed routes, as long as the points are not overlong so that the decision as to which crampons to buy probably comes down to whether ice pitches are going to be climbed. One instance where hinged crampons may be necessary is that where a small boot size is involved, particularly a lady's boot which may have a greater curvature of sole.

If step-in bindings are bought, they must be used with a safety ankle strap. Bad enough losing a crampon, disastrous to see it tumble down the slope. If using crampons with straps, the best uses two straps per crampon, one for the heel section which goes round the ankle, the other for the front section going over the foot. The strap material should be neoprene or other waterproof and non-freezing material, with a simple but virtually foolproof pin and buckle

Crampons

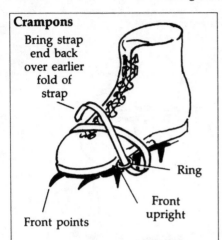

Bring strap end back over earlier fold of strap

Ring

Front upright

Front points

5. Some crampon straps do not use a toe ring, instead running through toe rings on the front uprights of the crampon. In this case, the crampon straps should always be run through the front rings from the outside to the inside. When brought back over the lower strap, this helps to prevent the lower strap from sliding forwards over the toe of the boot.

type of fastening. The crampon should be adjusted so that it fits snugly to the boot; you should be able to pick the boot and crampon up and without having fastened the straps be unable to shake off the crampon. The front points should project beyond each toe about 2–3cm. Do not be surprised if there are slight differences between left and right boots, and between left and right points.

Step-in bindings rely on metal bars clicking into rebates on the toe and heels of the boots. New plastic boots will have these shelves, old or leather boots may not be as conveniently made, so take in boots when buying crampons. It goes without saying that step-in bindings must fit perfectly. They may require adjustment following the first fitting, so allow for this and perhaps try them out on an easy route first.

If using straps for attachment and fitting them at home, follow maker's instructions carefully, particularly if any riveting is involved, as this tends to be a committing process. Buckles are always placed on the outside of boots, so as not to foul on the other boot. The strap goes through the front crampon rings from the outside to the inside, providing a self-locking mechanism.

In wet snow all crampons can be prey to *balling-up*, particularly the rigid types. This is the attachment of snow to the underside of crampons in mild weather, forming compacted lumps which are potentially danger-ous since they can cause a climber to stumble or slide, as the crampon points may not then be biting into the slope. Balling-up can be removed by striking the crampons a hard tap using the shaft of the ice axe, or pre-venting by the insertion of a piece of thick plastic sheeting or nylon between the crampons and the soles of the boots. This will quickly wear out however, especially on a *mixed route*. The Messner step-ins have an attachable flat rubber sheet, shaped to fit under the boot sole and hook-ing on to the crampon frame.

Unless removing and replacing crampons constantly, the best place to carry them when not actually wearing them is inside the *rucksack* with rubber protectors covering the points to prevent damage. On the top of a rucksack, and especially in the wrong hands, they can easily cause damage and even injury to other climbers. Maintenance of crampons should involve a regular check, and certainly a careful one at the begin-ning of the season. Check the tight-ness of all nuts and screws. Check points for bluntness and burrs and attend to these with a hand file for a few minutes. The amount of filing done will depend on the amount of ice climbed. A regular climber on ice and mixed routes will have to touch up points more often. Over-sharpening is to be avoided. Use a hand file only and sharpen the down points to a point, and the front points to a chisel point. Finally check the straps, their rivets and buckles. If heavily worn replace before they snap on a route, with potentially lethal consequences. (For climbing with crampons see *front pointing*.)

Crevasse. Cracks in a *glacier*, caused by movement of the ice. They may be anything from a few metres to many in depth, and may be hidden by snow or open and obvious. In the high mountains, which have glaciers, there is usually a seasonal variation in the amount of snow cover found on a glacier, from a heavy cover in the winter which can obscure many crevasses, to a virtually dry or snowless glacier in the autumn. Snow may provide a safe bridge over a glacier, or it may provide a trap. See *glacier travel* and *crevasse rescue*.

Crevasse rescue. Many Alpine routes require crossing or travelling on a *glacier*, with the necessity of being prepared for falling into, and escaping from, a *crevasse*. This preparation, which involves moving while roped together, requires a knowledge of rope coiling, knot tying, snow belaying, the use of *crampons*, and *prusiking*. The safest number for moving over a crevassed area is three or four, but it is possible to safeguard such travel for a pair of climbers, which is, of course, the normal climbing unit.

Start preparations for glacier travel by roping up — a single rope is convenient, and the other rope can then be carried by one of the team. There should be at least 10m of rope between partners, so both will have to coil about 16m of rope (several metres are always taken up by knots).

The coils will probably be made over the rucksack, which makes removing it while roped up difficult if not impossible. Begin coiling the rope under the arm and over the shoulder, giving a smaller coil than usual for rope coiling. About a dozen or so coils will probably do. Pull a bight of the live rope up and under the coils. The length of the bight should allow it to reach down to just below the waist. With the bight tie a *figure-of-eight* knot, taking in the live rope. The final loop on the knot should be as neat as possible and just reach the harness screw-gate karabiner, to which it is then connected. Given that the shoulder coils are snug and that there is little slack in the set-up, there should now be a rudimentary body harness for both climbers, with at least 10m of rope between. The middle man, if there is one, can tie on using a figure-of-eight knot, allowing about 10m of rope to separate each climber.

The second stage is to prepare the *prusik* loops. There should be two loops, a shorter loop for the harness, and a longer leg loop. The leg loop is attached lower down the rope, with both loops being attached fairly close to the harness. The extra length of the leg loop is an inconvenience, and can be kept in a pocket unless needed. When moving together, the leader should not have to worry about the rope, that being the task, as during climbing itself, of the second. So the rope goes back from the leader to the second, who keeps it taut and out of the way. The second should also have at least one long sling and karabiner handy for belaying. This task can be eased by using the harness prusik loop as a convenient handle — there should be no coils of rope held in the hand by either climber, in contrast to moving together on a mountain route. This

Crevasse rescue

1. *Preparing the rope for crevasse travel. Begin coiling the rope round one shoulder, using small coils.*

2. *When about a dozen or so coils have been formed, pull a bight of the 'live' rope up and under the coils.*

Crevasse rescue

3. The bight should be long enough that it reaches just below the waist.

Live rope

4 & 5. With the bight, tie a figure-of-eight knot, taking in the live rope.

Crevasse rescue

6. The final loop on the figure-of-eight knot should be as neat as possible, and should just be able to be clipped into the harness screwgate karabiner.

If using a harness which does not normally require a karabiner, it will be necessary to use one, linking the figure-of-eight knot loop with the tie-in knot.

7. Preparing a belay for a fallen partner.

Once an axe belay has been made by burying the axe horizontally (see belay diagrams 9, 10 & 11) then a second axe, if available, can be used to reinforce the first, by placing it vertically behind the first. Connect the two axes using a clove hitch knot. A rucksack, also buried horizontally, will make a sufficiently good belay, especially if well covered and firmed down.

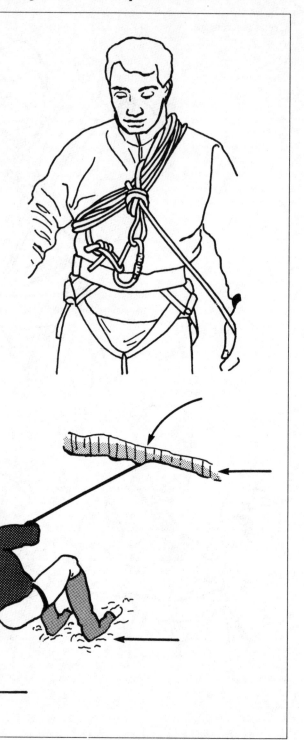

will minimize the distance fallen should either climber plunge into a crevasse. Wear crampons, even if the snow is *balling-up* — under such conditions a crevasse may open up to swallow a climber, and crampons may make escape much easier.

Obviously it is far better to avoid falling into a crevasse in the first place, so choose the route over the glacier carefully. It may be that a well-worn path is present. Follow this if it is in daily use but be prepared for crevasses in any case. If a professionally guided party is seen they will almost certainly be following a safe route. The middle of a glacier is often the safest. Avoid icefalls, and if in doubt about a section, perhaps because of a suspicious hollow on the surface, probe it using an axe. It may be necessary or convenient, to leap over a small crevasse. *Snow bridges* may be found crossing a crevasse, varying from the small and frightening to the huge and frightening. Before jumping or crossing, the second should take a belay, which may be a simple sitting belay with feet well dug-in, or a more secure belay using an *axe belay*. The leader making a jump can hold several coils in hand to prevent them snagging on crampon points, releasing them mid-jump. Crossing a delicate-looking snow bridge may require a cautious crawl, to distribute weight as much as possible. Just because the leader makes a successful crossing it does not invalidate the necessity of some sort of a belay for the second.

If precautions fail and the leader decides to explore the depths of a crevasse then the second must immediately begin emergency procedures. Assuming well dug-in feet, aided probably by an axe, wait to see if the leader can emerge using prusiks. There will normally be sufficient friction to allow the second to

hold without too much of a struggle. It may not be possible to communicate right away, due to the sound-deadening effects of snow and ice, but a movement on the rope is usually a good indication, assuming that the leader was prepared of course.

If time goes by and nothing seems to be happening assume the worst and start preparing a belay. This will secure the fallen climber and allow the second to approach the crevasse. Still digging in with heels cut a slot behind big enough to hold an axe horizontally and preferably a rucksack as well. If using a sack, remember to remove the spare rope first, if that is where it is kept. None of this will be easy, given the necessity of holding on to the live rope but persist. Attach the end of the long prusik loop to a sling with a karabiner then the sling to the axe using a *clove hitch* or round the rucksack, which will provide a better belay, being that much bigger. Now bury axe or sack with attached sling as deeply and firmly as possible. If a second axe is available it may be used in conjunction with the first to greatly improve an axe belay. Push it down vertically, behind the horizontal axe, so as to form a T-shape, and connect the two axes with the sling using a clove hitch.

Once the belay is fixed slide the prusik knot down the live rope until the prusik loop is tight. Gently move towards the crevasse so that the loading is transferred to the belay. You can now, assuming the belay is holding, untie from the rope at your harness. To make the belay even more secure, tie a figure-of-eight knot in the rope above a prusik, then secure that to the belay. If spare rope is available make a separate belay, given enough gear, and safeguard the approach to the crevasse edge. Failing a second belay carefully use the prepared belay, using the harness prusik as a moving belay in either case.

If the fallen climber is uninjured and able to prusik then the situation should resolve itself. If unconscious or unable to prusik then with a party of two there is a serious situation. It may be possible, with a major effort and an extra prusik, to haul out the hapless victim. Belay and escape from the live rope will be as before. If possible, the edge of the crevasse where the rope runs down to the victim should be prepared so as to minimize friction. Carefully cut a box for the rope and reinforce the edge with some item of gear — sack, anorak, anything which will ease the rope's passage upwards. The original prusik securing the live rope will have to be replaced with an inverted *Bachmann knot*. Now tie a short prusik loop to the live rope below the Bachmann and clip a karabiner into this new prusik. The karabiner on the belay is going to act as a pulley, giving a little but much-needed mechanical advantage. Clip the free rope into the prusik karabiner. When the free rope is pulled, the live rope will move up until the Bachmann karabiner jams against the belay. On releasing the free rope, the Bachmann should hold the live rope, allowing the prusik to be slid down the live rope, ready for the next haul. By now it is obvious why three on a rope is best for glacier travel.

Crux. The hardest move, or sequence of moves, on a route. A climb will be awarded a technical grade based on the crux, whereas the overall grade will take into account protection and other factors.

Dachstein. Woollen mitts used for winter walking and climbing. Austrian made, these mitts are manufac-tured large then shrunk down to hand-size, making them thick and warm even in very cold conditions. In wet or extremely severe conditions they can be used in conjunction with waterproof *overmitts*. The thumb is provided with its own compartment, an arrangement which is warmer than a glove with separate fingers, as in a mitt the fingers gain some heat from adjacent fingers.

Dagger. Winter climbing tool now replaced by front pointing axes. Used especially by Continental climbers in combination with an axe, the dagger was stabbed into the snow or ice and used as a hand hold. Some designs resembled a potato peeler, with the blade having a V-shaped cross section.

Deadman. An extremely effective snow belay, consisting of a thin alloy plate, rectangular in shape with the lower end gently pointed and the upper end reinforced to take hammer blows without distorting. The plate is about 20 by 25cm with a strong wire cable connected to its centre. The plate is lightened with drilled out openings. Smaller versions known as deadboys are also available. For method of use see *belay*.

Descender. An alloy device used for abseiling and other techniques. The most universal model is the *figure-of-eight*. It is also possible to use a *belay plate*, especially when the rope is wet and friction is reduced, and a *karabiner brake* using two screwgate karabiners. Other types of descender include the Petzl Stop, which incorporates a clever 'deadman's hand' lever. This is pressed gently while descending, but if the hand is removed for some reason, either deliberately or through accident, the descender locks, preventing further

Deadman

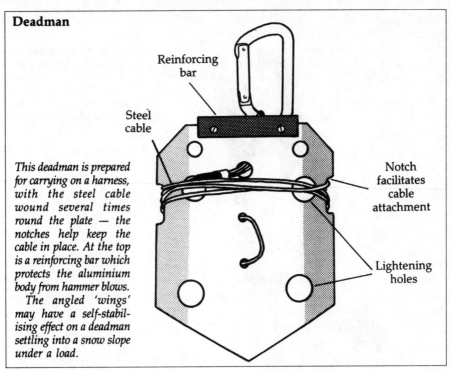

Reinforcing bar

Steel cable

Notch facilitates cable attachment

Lightening holes

This deadman is prepared for carrying on a harness, with the steel cable wound several times round the plate — the notches help keep the cable in place. At the top is a reinforcing bar which protects the aluminium body from hammer blows.

The angled 'wings' may have a self-stabil-ising effect on a deadman settling into a snow slope under a load.

Descender

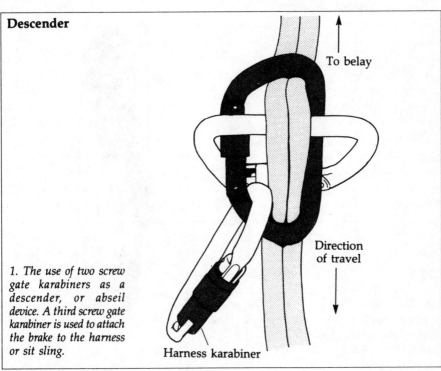

To belay

Direction of travel

Harness karabiner

1. The use of two screw gate karabiners as a descender, or abseil device. A third screw gate karabiner is used to attach the brake to the harness or sit sling.

Descender

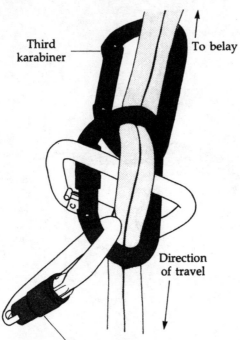

Third
karabiner

To belay

2. *If extra friction is desired, perhaps because the ropes are wet, then an extra, third karabiner may be added to the arrangement as shown.*

Direction
of travel

Harness karabiner

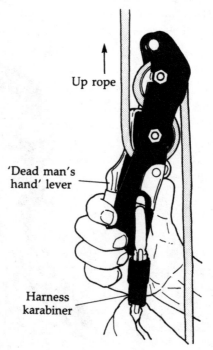

Up rope

'Dead man's
hand' lever

Harness
karabiner

3. *The Petzl Stop descender, in the sliding position, with the controlling hand on the 'dead man's hand' lever.*

Descender

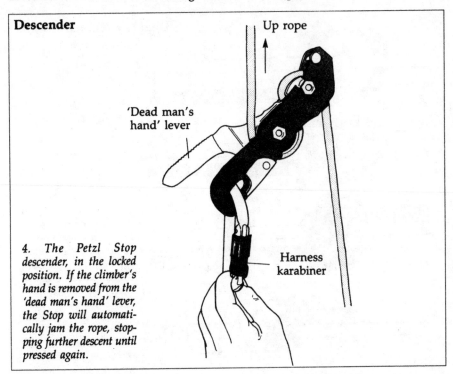

Up rope

'Dead man's hand' lever

Harness karabiner

4. The Petzl Stop descender, in the locked position. If the climber's hand is removed from the 'dead man's hand' lever, the Stop will automatically jam the rope, stopping further descent until pressed again.

descent until pressed again. A descender can be useful for lowering or for belaying when the loading will not be great, eg, during *top roping*. See *abseil*.

Dièdre. See *corner*.

Diet. If you are aiming for the top grades of the sport then it is intelligent to analyse your diet. A badly overweight climber is a rarity, while some ambitious but overlean athletes might consider putting on a little weight in the form of muscle. This would require, apart from the obvious exercising, a sufficient intake of good quality protein, perhaps in the form of some of the many powdered drinks available. A balanced diet is necessary whatever the aim, with a sufficient intake of vitamins and minerals. The average British or American diet is appalling, with too much animal fat, too little fresh fruit

and vegetables. Like exercise, a good diet may not allow you to live much longer, but it will allow you to enjoy the years you have. Eat well in the days prior to undertaking any strenuous climbing, to stock up the body's reserves. Ethics besides, many have found that going vegetarian has improved performance. Avoid anything in excess, including *alcohol*. Some climbers even increase the odds against longevity by smoking.

Food carried while climbing is obviously required to maintain energy levels, especially important during winter and/or in bad weather. Health bars, mixed nuts, cake, chocolate bars, sandwiches are all good, with fruit thrown in to quench thirst and help sustain fluid levels. A *water bottle* can be carried usefully all year round, with water or some fruit juice. There can be dehydration in winter, despite being surrounded by frozen water. Keep readily available food in

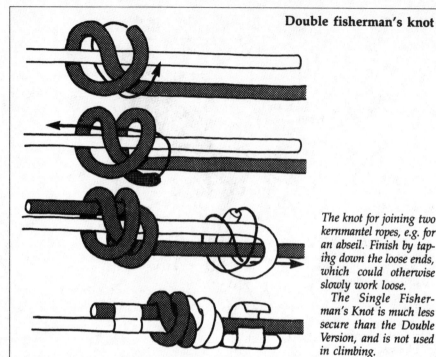

Double fisherman's knot

The knot for joining two kernmantel ropes, e.g. for an abseil. Finish by tapihg down the loose ends, which could otherwise slowly work loose.

The Single Fisherman's Knot is much less secure than the Double Version, and is not used in climbing.

an anorak pocket, useful for quick mouthfuls through the day. A low energy level can hit one quickly, better to eat a little at regular intervals than wait all day for a big lunch. A thermos flask with a hot drink is good in winter, if you can be bothered to carry the extra weight.

Dinner plating. The fracturing of ice when struck with an axe, causing plate-shaped fragments to break off. Can also occur when inserting an *ice screw*. Normally only found with *water ice*. Can sometimes make it impossible to arrange good protection. Care should be taken when front pointing, as a pick could come out on moving up past a fractured section of ice. Look out for cracks in the ice when inserting a pick.

Double fisherman's knot. This is the strongest knot available for tying together two ropes, eg, in order to

make an abseil (59% in 9mm rope). Also for making rope slings. It is relatively bulky and requires more rope than the single version. Tape off the end for security. Known as a *Grapevine knot* in the USA.

Double rope technique. The use of two ropes in climbing a route. Many beginning climbers use a single, 11mm rope. This is safe and adequate for the easier routes, and also more economical if shared between two climbers. Once multi-pitch, more complex routes are encountered however, the advantages of using two ropes become evident. Normally two 45m, 9mm diameter ropes will be used. In winter there is occasional advantage in using 50m ropes for longer runouts, though these are not strictly necessary. Ropes should be coloured differently for quick and easy identification. The main advantages of two ropes over a single rope

Double rope technique

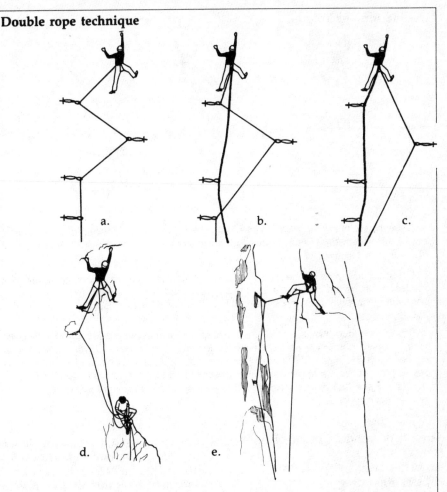

a.   b.   c.

d.   e.

a. *Using a single rope, with runners spaced out to left and right, a climber is forced to either ignore some runners, e.g. number three in this example, or use it with the risk of having rope drag due to the angles the rope is obliged to undergo. The rope will also have a much higher risk of jamming in cracks, over flakes and overhangs, etc.*

b. *Using a double rope, the correct order of using the four available runners is not a strictly alternating one. This has given rise to, in this wrongly executed example, ropes crossing over each other, as well as a sharp angle of turn for one of the ropes using runner number three.*

c. *The correct use of double ropes. Keeping them apart, with the left hand rope using runners one, two and four, and the right hand rope using runner three only.*

d. *Climber, just starting out on a wall pitch, has placed the first runner using one rope. The next runner will probably be used by the other rope, unless to do so would cause rope drag.*

e. *Climber here is keeping the ropes apart by using one rope for runners on the left of the corner, and waiting until a runner appears on the right before using the other rope.*

Double rope technique

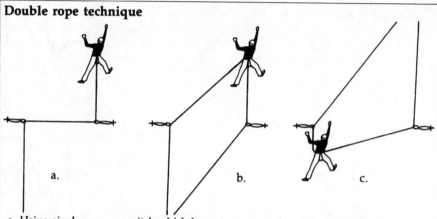

a. Using single rope on a pitch which has a traverse section, it is very difficult to protect the second. When the second removes runner number one, he or she will be faced with a bad swing in the event of a fall.

b. Using a double rope, and keeping the two ropes to their respective runners, by the time the leader has gained a higher belay the second should be well protected on the traverse, even after removing runner number two, with only a small swing in the event of a fall.

c. If there is a long traverse, as in this example, the second can employ a back rope technique, keeping runner one on until reaching the end of the traverse. If the runner has to be abandoned, the rope will be untied (leave no knot!), pulled up by the leader, and perhaps passed back down again to the second who can then retie back into the rope. Obviously, during the use of a back rope, the leader will be paying out the rope running through runner one, and taking in the other rope.

are, in descending order of importance:

a) better arranged protection
b) less rope drag
c) longer abseils possible
d) fewer arguments as to who carries the rope!

Protecting a pitch using a single rope can lead to problems when runners are found on either side of the main line of ascent. The rope may have to zigzag up the pitch, or miss out runners. Even using long slings or extenders on the runners, rope drag can build up very quickly as the main climbing rope is forced round and over obstacles. A leader can quite literally be pulled to a halt on a long, tortuous pitch. With a double rope, runners are preferably clipped into alternate ropes, with ideally, one rope being used for the same line of runners. On a climb with a linear feature such as a crack, the ropes will obviously be running together for some distance. Both ropes may then be clipped into the same runner if wished, and certainly it is advisable if there is a long distance between runners. Obviously it is possible that a leader will fall some distance with only a single, 9mm rope taking most of the force. Modern ropes are designed to absorb a high load, and unless there is a very high *fall factor* and particularly unlucky circumstances, the rope should not break.

The second will also benefit from better protection using double ropes, particularly if the pitch contains a traverse section. With a single rope, a second's fall at the start of a traverse may mean a long swing, which can be prevented by using a double rope.

Double rope technique is slightly more demanding on rope management than single, as ropes can be twisted, crossed or become hopelessly bundled up in one giant mess of 'knitting'. Lessen the chances of a mess by keeping the ropes apart when uncoiling, tying on, taking in etc. Think ahead when leading, as it is easy to place a runner in the wrong spot, possibly lifting out another runner for example. Good double rope technique should come with experience, with its application being one of the pleasures of safe climbing.

Drag. Friction generated by a rope running over rock features, jamming in cracks etc. Minimized by using a *double rope* and by careful placement of protection.

Drive in. Type of ice screw which is hammered or driven in, and removed by unscrewing. It is solid and narrower than a tubular screw, and therefore has less holding power, but it is quickly inserted and has saved many a tired leader. A popular make, known as a wart hog, has lines of 'warts' or projections, running down the screw in a spiral to facilitate removal. When placing a screw, clear away any loose surface material. Drive the screw in to its limit, at an angle of about 80 degrees to the slope. The drive in should not be tied off, due to its lower holding power, though if nothing else exists for protection at that point who is to argue. In areas of the world where frozen turf is a valuable asset to a winter ascent, a drive in provides a very secure runner or belay when driven into the turf.

Duvet. A warm jacket filled with an insulating material such as goose down or, more recently, some synthetic material. Too warm to climb with in any but the most severe climatic conditions, a duvet is useful for Alpine bivouacs, winter camping etc. Some duvets are also waterproof.

Dyno. To make a dynamic leap for a hold which otherwise could not be reached, perhaps due to a lack of intermediate holds. This is a committing process and demands confidence.

Eliminate line. A direct ascent of a rock or mountain feature, or of an earlier route, normally more difficult than the original as it misses out or 'eliminates' easy sections such as traverses. These eliminates, or variations, may be anything from a few moves to several pitches in length.

Ethics. Climbing is somewhat unusual in that it is a sport practised with no written rules. Apart from the occasional individual, and attempts by some groups (notably Soviet climbers), it is not an overtly competitive sport. This narrows the competition to a more personal level, so that to cheat is to cheat oneself, thereby reducing the amount of cheating to a very minor level. Using aid on a free route is cheating. Using a bolt runner where good protection is available is cheating. Other infringements of ethics may be more difficult to define, but a climber is normally aware of what is generally regarded as good 'style' for an ascent. It has recently become poor style, for example, to attempt a major Himalayan peak with a hundred porters, the present style being to attempt it in Alpine fashion, with climbers carrying most, or all of the equipment.

The general trend is for aid to be reduced, and the mountain or route to be left as far as possible in its original state, other than necessary *gardening*. Thus the controversy when *chalk* began to be used, as it left a visible trail on the rock, but a lack of controversy when 'sticky' rock boots appeared, even though they made climbing easier. In a similar vein, *front pointing* was not contested, probably because although it made winter climbing safer and easier, it left the routes in a state approaching their untouched condition, better for the next party to climb. Ethics are evolving continually. The current problem under discussion involves the use of bolts on rock climbs. These can be placed anywhere, by abseil, so that the rock is overwhelmed by technology. They do allow otherwise poorly protected rock to be climbed safely, however, and given discipline their use on a small scale will probably continue for the immediate future.

Etriers. Short lengths of portable steps, normally about three, used for *aid climbing*. They are made either of nylon tape, knotted if home-made, sewn if bought (with stiffer tape easier to use), or as alloy rungs drilled at each end so as to allow accessory rope to be fitted. A loop at the top allows a karabiner and/or a *fifi hook* to be attached. In aid climbing, étriers clipped into a peg or other attachment point on the rock allow a climber to move up otherwise impossible rock, perhaps because it overhangs, or has no holds. The étriers are moved up alternately, with the climber using as high a step as possible to allow the next aid point to be fixed. While standing on one of the steps of an étrier, a line from the **harness** can also be clipped into the aid point, so that the climber can remain with no effort at that point.

Expedition. To a young beginner almost any trip to the mountains may be regarded as an 'expedition'. However, it is generally accepted that an expedition involves a trip by a party of mountaineers to some fairly remote part of the world. The trip will normally entail some length of approach by foot, though some parts of the world, eg, Alaska, are accessible by light plane. As very few climbing millionaires are about, some form of sponsorship to raise funding for an expedition is normally part of the work involved in organizing an expedition, with industry and perhaps the media being involved. There also exist various bodies which have funds set by for such trips, lists of whom should be available from the national mountaineering councils. The recent trend has been towards smaller, more personal expeditions.

In planning an expedition some sort of leadership is often an advantage, even if only as a name on headed notepaper. It helps to have one or two 'big names' in the background, for advice and to help impress potential sponsors, who are quite rightly expecting some sort of return for their money. The various tasks can be allocated to individual members of the expedition, who are then responsible for carrying through the planning. Permission to climb may often be required from a country, as well as a possible fee and proof of adequate insurance cover. Talk to climbers who have been on previous expeditions; a short conversation can prevent mistakes being repeated, and begin planning about two years in advance for certain countries.

Exposure. a) The awareness or feeling of a large drop beneath a climber, found particularly on steep walls. This is part of the fun of a route or section of a route, as long as it is kept under control!

b) Layman's term for hypothermia. A potentially serious condition caused by a drop in core body temperature, often due to bad weather and/or fatigue. Inadequate clothing and cold, wet conditions are common contributory factors. Progressive signs to be looked for in a victim (who will be unaware of the condition) are lethargy, unreasonable behaviour, slurring of speech, vision disorders, collapse, unconsciousness. If core temperature continues to drop arrythymia sets in, leading eventually to fibrillation and death. Rumour has it that it is a relatively pleasant death, like dropping off to sleep, once the initial shivery stage has been passed. Emergency treatment is immediate shelter from the elements, with placement into a *bivouac bag* or sleeping bag. If exposure is severe a friend should be in the same bag to provide body heat. Best of all is to learn to recognize exposure conditions, maintain good body stores of energy by proper and frequent ingestion of food, and by being fit and avoiding unnecessary fatigue, particularly in bad weather. See *wind-chill*.

Extenders. Also known as *Quick Draws, Snake Slings, Screamers* and *Hero Loops.* Devised by the American climber Bill Forrest and first used in the Yosemite Valley, these are nylon tape slings whose main use is in conjunction with a runner, especially small *wires* which might easily be dislodged by movement of the main rope. Extenders come in several lengths and widths; usually between 10 and 25cm in finished length, and 12 to 25mm width. They may be made up by the climber, in which case they will be knotted, or bought pre-stitched. Stitched slings are best. Recently developed models of extenders such as the DMM 'Screamer' have folded sections stitched together, so that under a loading they will gradually extend as the stitches are ripped, theoretically reducing the loading on a small or dubious runner. These could have a use in winter, with ice screws. Extenders should be used for wired nuts only in combination with a karabiner, as the small diameter wire could quite easily cut through a sling under loading. The ends of the loops on several models of extenders, eg, those by Petzl, are narrowed, having been rolled; this reduces the loading on a karabiner. Extenders are often carried ready on the harness with two karabiners attached, one for the runner and one through which the climbing rope will pass. See *kernmantel*.

Falls. A fall while climbing may occur due to a number of reasons. The route may be technically beyond your capability, or too strenuous. You may be unfit, or having a day when for reasons unknown you are below par. Until recently, to fall was bad news; protection was poor, equipment rudimentary, the embarrassment maximum. In winter protection may remain minimal on some routes and a fall is still unwanted, but in rock climbing, particularly towards the higher grades, falls are accepted by many leaders as part of the learning process, necessary to force new standards and unknown cruxes. This acceptance is realizable solely due to great improvements in protection equipment. It is not a good practice for the beginner to emulate however, as limited experience will lower protection efficiency. Paradoxically, it may be more dangerous to fall on easier routes, whose often easier angles make it more likely that a falling leader can strike rocks on the descent, rather than hang in mid-air on a hard route.

A fall may happen to anyone however. Bad rock, sudden rain, straying off-route can all lead to the ultimate test of your protection techniques. Sometimes there will be time to insert a runner before tiredness sets in. If secure enough, an exhausted leader can be lowered from this until the belay or some resting place can be reached. Do not try and save a little money and be tempted to thread the rope through a sling instead of leaving the karabiner, no economies are worth a healthy life. A rope running through a nylon sling can burn its way through very quickly due to friction. An awkward moment can happen if a fall leaves a leader or second hanging free due to an overhang. If lowering is not possible then prusik loops will have to be manufactured for *self-rescue*. For reasons described below in *fall factor*, it is important to put in runners very soon after leaving the belay. A properly fitting harness is also necessary, to protect and cushion vital organs during a fall, and to prevent asphyxiation if hanging free following one.

Fall factor. The ratio of the length of fall to the length of rope run out. The maximum possible factor is one of 2, as for example when a leader who has no runners on falls while 10m above the belay. As the fall will be 20m (10m to the belay then 10m below it) and 10m of rope has been run out, then

$$\text{Fall factor} = \frac{10 + 10}{10} = 2$$

This is the worst possible loading for a rope, and though modern climbing ropes have been designed for the worst, avoid putting them to this test! Equal fall factors will produce the same maximum force on the rope and/or belay system, so that even a relatively short fall close to the belay can be traumatic if a high fall factor is present.

Fifi hook. Metal hook attached to the top of an *étrier*, allowing the étrier to be clipped into a *peg* or some other attachment point on a route. A small hole on the top of the fifi allows a thin accessory cord to be tied on. When attached to the harness, the étrier is safeguarded from being lost if dropped.

Figure-of-eight. a) Popular *abseil* device, two rings of alloy joined like the numeral eight. The smaller ring attaches to the climbing harness using a *screw gate karabiner*, while in use the rope runs through and round the larger ring. The descent is controlled by varying the angle of the controlling, or lower rope. The lower down this is held, and the more parallel it is to the upper rope, the greater the friction. More friction means a slower descent, with the energy generated by a descending climber being dissipated as heat through the figure-of-eight. Bringing the controlling rope up towards the upper rope means less friction. Can also be useful as a belaying device, though not providing as much friction as a *belay plate*. Other makes of figures-of-eight include the Anka by DMM, which does not lead to rope twist, and the Kong by Bonaiti, which has a small extension for attaching an accessory cord to. **Tip**. Be careful if abseiling with wet ropes, especially during a fall of wet snow. The friction may be much reduced, leading to a too rapid rate of descent. Use a belay plate in such conditions. b) A useful knot, easy to tie, and used for attachment to belay anchors and for attachment to the middle of a rope, eg, when moving together as a threesome. Has a knot strength, in 9mm rope, of about 62%.

Fingerboard. See *training*.

First aid. It should be the personal responsibility of each participant in any potentially dangerous sport to learn at least the rudiments of basic first aid. A small first aid kit can live in the rucksack, and could hold plasters, soluble aspirin, and perhaps a bandage or two. More important is knowing how to ensure that an injured climber continues to breathe following some trauma. Skilled help will probably be hours away. What seems straightforward on the living-room carpet can be desperately confusing on a winter night with snow blowing and a messy accident victim to examine. Keep your head. First check the breathing. If not breathing then make sure that the airway is clear of blood, vomit, snow etc — free it using a finger if necessary. If still not breathing then resuscitation will have to be undertaken. Learn the technique from an expert. If the heart has stopped (best place to check for pulse is at the side of the neck) then heart massage will have to alternate with mouth-to-mouth. This is best done with two rescuers, continuing until the victim breathes spontaneously, or for at least thirty minutes if not.

Unless a spinal injury is suspected, gently turn the unconscious victim into the recovery position, which is the easiest breathing position. Now look for severe bleeding and stem this if possible. Use pressure on folded clothing and raise a bleeding limb to reduce the flow. Check for broken bones and use slings etc for immobilizing limbs. Prevent *hypothermia*. Organize some shelter from the wind, break out spare clothing, *space blankets*, *bivvy bags*, food etc. Make regular checks on the victim and reassure often if conscious.

The particular circumstances of

Figure-of-eight

1. *Three figures-of-eight, used for abseiling and/or belaying. The principle is the same in all models. The small ring is attached to the harness, after a bight of the rope is taken round it, having first taken the bight through the larger ring. The Camp model, centre, has a tiny side ring for attaching a safety cord to, while the DMM Anka model, bottom, has the added benefit of keeping the two ropes separate.*

Figure-of-eight

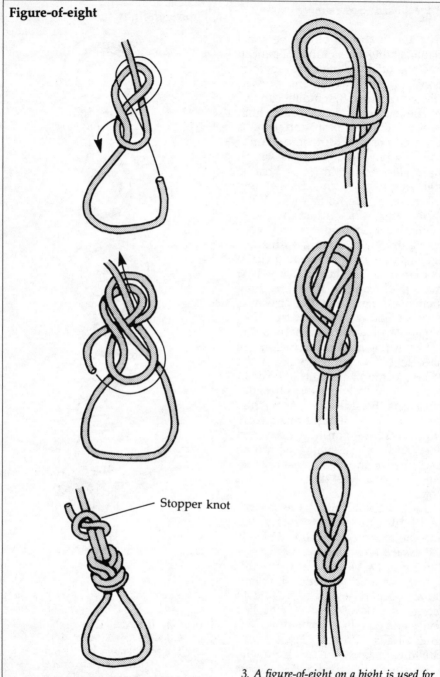

Stopper knot

2. A figure-of-eight knot, finished off with a single stopper knot. This is a knot commonly used for tying into a harness.

3. A figure-of-eight on a bight is used for tying into a belay karabiner, or for a middle climber on a rope of three, e.g. when traversing a glacier.

Figure-of-eight

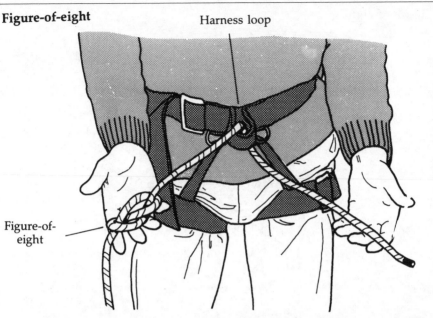

Harness loop

Figure-of-eight

4. *Tying into a Pat Littlejohn harness using a figure-of-eight knot. First tie a figure-of-eight in the rope, then thread the end of the rope through the harness loop or loops, according to the maker's instructions.*

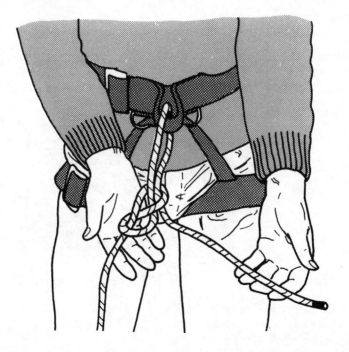

5. *Thread the end of the rope through the knot, following the original loop.*

Figure-of-eight

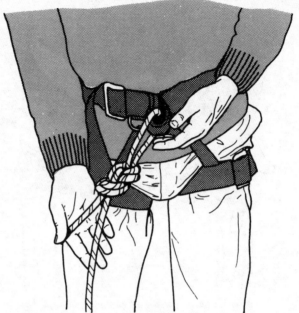

6. *Continue threading the rope...*

7. *...until it emerges below the knot.*

Figure-of-eight

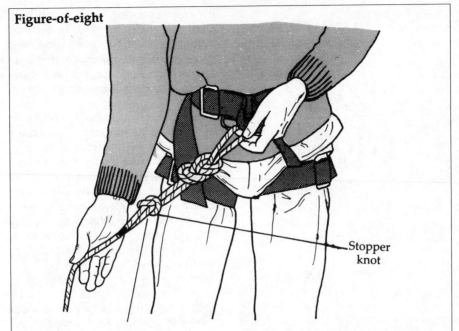

Stopper
knot

8. Tie it off with a stopper knot, made up closer to the main knot than in the illustration shown here.

each accident will determine how help is sought. First aid comes first however, unless there is a spare member or members of the party who can seek aid simultaneously. Make sure the precise position is agreed upon. Change may be needed for a telephone call. Spare torch batteries may be better left with the injured.

First ascents. The climbing of a route for the first time. This may also be the first winter ascent of an already existing summer line or more rarely, the converse. To make a first ascent is normally more demanding than making a subsequent one, as often little will be known of the route, other than a general estimate of its overall difficulties. Additionally, there may be vegetation and loose rock, adding to the difficulties. An exception to this is with the hardest rock climbs, where a first ascent party may have

spent considerable time working out the route while the second ascent party will have to attempt the route with much less knowledge.

The shorter summer routes in the hard grades are now often examined by abseil before attempting an ascent, with excess vegetation being scrubbed off using a wire brush and perhaps, with climbing close to the limit of personal ability in some cases, runners being placed before attempting the climb. The purist, and certainly the climber on easier routes, will in all probability make the ascent from the ground up with no prior inspection or *gardening*. The first ascender normally has the privilege of naming the new route, which can then be recorded in a number of sources, depending on its geographical locality. The major mountaineering club journals are the sensible places for recording new routes, as the same clubs will also be responsi-

Foot brake

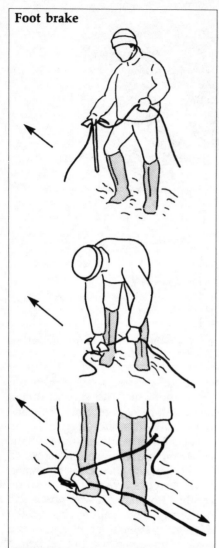

Foot brake for winter climbing, using the ice axe only.

1. *Position the front, uphill boot in the snow and push or hammer in the axe vertically above it (climber seen from front, facing across slope).*

2. *Run the rope or ropes behind the axe, and arrange it so that the ropes run over the boot. The lower, downhill hand controls the ropes, the uphill hand presses down on the axe head. Extra friction may be gained by pulling back the ropes over more of the boot ankle.*

ble for updating and publishing climbing *guides* to their areas. First ascents are satisfying, exciting, and given the rule of quality coming first, are perhaps necessary for the continuance of the evolution of the sport.

Fixed rope. A rope attached to part of a route on a mountain, especially on popular Alpine routes, to safeguard and make easier difficult passages. They may be more permanent erections of metal. In the Himalaya, ascents of the high peaks by an expedition may be facilitated by the use of fixed ropes, allowing loads to be carried between camps. *Jumar* clamps are then used when moving up a fixed rope, giving some degree of protection against a slip. They do not help though if an avalanche removes the belay or rope, or if a rope wears through due to abrasion.

Flake. A spike or flake of rock partly attached to a rock face. A flake may be soundly attached, or semi-detached, when it may sometimes be detected by moving slightly or by having a hollow sound when struck with a fist. Very small flakes, though often providing good handholds, should always be treated with caution as they may snap under load. Most climbers will have had this experience, some falling as a result. Flakes may provide good runners, with a sling being placed round the flake. Tape slings can fit behind thin flake cracks more easily than accessory loops.

Flash. To climb a route without falls or lowers to rest, though it is permitted to have prior knowledge of the crux, protection etc, perhaps gained from an abseil.

Foot brake. A fast alternative to the *axe belay* on moderately-angled snow slopes. Push the axe vertically down into the snow, as far as the head. Facing across the fall line, kick the uphill boot in below and against the axe. The boot is there to prevent the axe being pulled out. Next, run the ropes round the axe shaft and arrange it so that both down and up sides lie over the boot. The boot will provide much of the friction. The uphill hand now presses down on the axe head, while the downhill hand controls the rope movement. The weight should be concentrated on the uphill foot and hand. If more friction is needed, such as when the second slips, the rope can be brought partly round the ankle of the uphill boot. Inferior to both the *deadman* and *bollard* belays, but may be adequate on easy ground and certainly very fast to arrange. Probably of use only for bringing up a second.

Free climbing. A route which involves no, or a minimum of, artificial aid. A long route with one or two points of aid, eg, a peg handhold and a pull on a sling might be regarded as a free route. A short route with four, five or more aid points on it will probably be looked on as an aid route. The aim is to completely eliminate aid points on a route, leading to its first free ascent. Many old *aid routes* have been freed, often utilizing old peg holes for hand holds.

Friends. See *camming devices*.

Front pointing. As hard snow or ice slopes become steeper, it no longer becomes easy to zig-zag up with both *crampons* flat on the slope. To some extent you can compromise, with one foot flat and a bent ankle, the other crampon with its front point kicked in. Alternating the feet when one leg becomes fatigued helps, this being a technique favoured by the French.

Eventually, however, one has to start front pointing. Front pointing in crampons involves facing in to the slope and kicking in the front points of the crampons. This technique was first developed in the 1920s by the Austrian and German climbers who had to contend with hard ice slopes on the north faces of their Eastern Alps.

All four points of each crampon are utilized in this technique; the two true front points, and the two points immediately behind these, which either face vertically down, or, in some models of crampons, at a slight angle forwards. In combination with kicking in the points, the axe picks will be used as temporary holds. The kicking should be positive but not violent, with the composition of the ice determining the security of the points. *Névé* will put up with almost any sloppy placement, while *water ice* demands greater care in placing the points. Water ice may require two or three kicks until you are satisfied with the placement.

The boots should be close to the horizontal; if you raise the heels muscle strain is induced while the front points may be tempted to shear out. Keep the feet still once placed. This is difficult at first, particularly as rock climbing usually allows a certain amount of foot play in the vertical plane. Be aware that on moving over bulges, which are common at the tops of pitches, your body may be leaning over but your feet should remain as they were placed until removed altogether.

The side points are not often used in front pointing snow and ice; they come into their own on buttress routes, where small rock holds may have to be used. Place the crampon on the chosen hold then keep it still, just as on ice. Once both feet have been placed select new pick placements. Do not be too ambitious with the stretch, overextending can lead to feet coming off. Select the pick placement and be positive in hitting it. It may be good first time or may require more than one blow before you are confident in its security. It is usually obvious when a good placement has been secured for the picks.

Arms work best and with the least amount of work when they are almost straight — when they have the 'athletic bend'. On very steep ground try and hang from your wrist loops with this slight bend in your arms. A common mistake, particularly before becoming warmed up and more relaxed, is to grip the shafts too firmly, tiring the hands. Once the picks are securely in place it's time for the feet to move up again, one at a time. It is possible on good ground to develop a rhythm, though in general front pointing steep ground is surprisingly jerky in practice.

On easy-angled ground you will find that to place the picks in while holding the shafts has you bending over the slope. This is unnecessary and impedes your breathing and view of the surroundings. Slide your hands up the shafts and push the picks in at right-angles to the slope, rather than hooking them in from below.

Arranging protection on steep ice is never straightforward. If a convenient break in the angle is present then use that to stand on while placing a *drive in* or *ice screw*. One small foothold may be cut if desired, though do not waste too much time doing this unless tired and needing a rest. The hammer pick will be doing the work of arranging protection. Assuming you are at the point where you wish to place a runner there are two ways of placing it. If you need the reassurance (and the rest!) then you can hang from the securely placed blade pick, with a short sling connecting your harness to the axe. More quickly, push your arm through the wrist loop of the axe, so that you can hold the screw or drive in and still be held by the axe. Either way, you can then begin the screw with a few taps of the hammer, finishing by screwing it in using the hammer pick as a ratchet, or by hammering in a drive in until firmly home. Clip in at once and pick in the hammer.

Frostbite. If extremities such as toes, fingers, nose, ear etc are subjected to very cold conditions, or even in less cold conditions with over-tight boots, small capillaries can be damaged and blood flow restricted, leading to more damage with thrombosis. Infection can set in at a later stage, particularly on an *expedition* far from good medical treatment. The first signs may be a loss of sensation and a loss of normal colour. Shelter and gentle warming of the affected tissues should be done as soon as possible. The return of circulation will be agonizing for a while, but is infinitely preferable to a permanent loss of circulation. No pain, no gain.

Gabbro. A volcanic rock type which has cooled slowly at depth and as a consequence has a coarse-grained, crystalline structure. It weathers roughly and is renowned for its roughness to the touch. Perhaps the best known exposure of gabbro in Britain is the superb Cuillin of Skye.

Gaiters. Nylon leg covering worn in winter for protection from snow and cold. Formerly made from canvas, gaiters run from just below the knees to cover the boot tops, and have a full-length zip usually on the front, which greatly facilitates their use. Some types of gaiter known as *Yetis* cover the entire boot as far as the top of the sole, with high-altitude models having an insulated lining for extra protection. These gaiters usually need to be glued down onto the boot to prevent them being pushed up in use. Most gaiters are provided with loops at the bottom to which a wire can be attached then run under the instep. This will prevent the gaiter from riding up in use, though in practice they are rarely needed. **Tips**. After a muddy walk, particularly over acid moorland, give the gaiters a thorough wash in running water to remove peaty material which can quickly rot some stitching. The running shoe repair material, known as 'Shoe Goo', is also excellent for gluing down gaiters and repairing small holes and tears.

Gangway. A sloping ledge on a rock face, often providing an easy route or section of a climb.

Gardening. The limited removal of vegetation from a rock climb, revealing holds and making an ascent easier. Many rock climbs follow natural lines of weakness such as cracks and chimneys. These will also be habitats for plant life, some of which may have to be removed by climbers often attempting a *first ascent*. Plants harbour moisture, collect soil, and may obscure holds. Climbers should be aware, however, that some plants may be protected due to their rarity, and should, in any case, keep gardening to the minimum necessary for making an ascent. Gardening of new, hard climbs is often done from abseil, using wire brushes and other tools to remove vegetation. **Tip**. Do your gardening then allow the weather, including heavy rain, to clean up the route. Disadvantage is that someone else might pinch your route!

Gendarme. A rock pinnacle found on a ridge, especially in the Alps. The size may vary from person-sized to the very large, perhaps causing a serious obstacle. Many can be avoided by climbing round their flanks. Some of the smaller ones can sit for years without moving then crash down with the next climber. Treat all with caution!

Girdle traverse. A route which for the most part climbs across a cliff, as opposed to the more normal upwards direction. Many girdles use naturally occurring ledge systems running across rock faces. There may be difficult sections involving *hand traverses*. They can provide much fun on the first ascent, but are not very popular with later climbers. Protection on a girdle has to be carefully worked out, as to fall might mean long pendulums or swings for either leader or second.

Glacier. A slow moving mass of ice found in the higher mountain ranges and in polar regions. The glaciers commonly met in the Alps will be fed by falling snow in the upper reaches which gradually changes to ice by a thawing and re-freezing process. Increasing depths of accumulating ice form and under the weight of overlying snow and ice the lowest layers are forced to flow downhill. The typical rate of flow is measured in centimetres per day, with the flow being highest in the middle. Differential rates of flow and the brittle nature of ice causes fracturing of the glacier in well-defined zones, eg, transverse and longitudinal *crevasses*. Glaciers are often disappointingly messy places carrying down shattered rocks, stones and mud. Long stripes of such debris are deposited as lateral *moraines*, while at the bottom end of the glacier may be a *terminal moraine*.

Glaciers which have little or no surface snow are referred to as dry glaciers. They are generally safer to walk over as most of the crevasses should be visible. One grisly reminder of both the danger and time scale of glaciers is the occasional finding, at the finish or mouth of a glacier, of the well-preserved and recognizable body of a *guide* or climber lost many years before further up the glacier. A posthumous journey of eighty years or so is not unknown. See *crevasse rescue*.

Glacier cream. Protection cream worn in high mountains and on glaciers to prevent burning from UV radiation and dehydration of facial. skin. On a glacier radiation can be reflected off the surface, giving a more intense burning effect. Burning can happen even on overcast days. *Lipsalves* should be used to prevent lips dehydrating. On high-altitude expeditions, goggles and nose shields may also be used, while even at lower altitudes eye damage may be prevented with good quality sunglasses, which should incorporate a UV filter.

Glissade. The rapid descent of a snow slope by a sliding, ski-like method, wearing boots. This is only recommended if the slope is safe, with the right consistency of snow (not too hard, not too soft), a safe runout, and no complications. A practised expert may even effect parallel turns. The dividing line, however, between a controlled glissade and an uncontrolled fall, is a narrow one. Obviously an axe must be carried and *braking* technique known.

Gloves. Hand coverings necessary for winter walking and climbing. The most commonly used gloves are woollen, fingerless mitts, especially of the *Dachstein* type. Ski-type fingered gloves are used by many Continental climbers with their colder, drier climate, though in wet, occasionally cold Britain, Dachsteins still rule. Either type of glove may be used in combination with an overmitt for bad conditions, of which the waterproof nylon type is best. For rock climbing in cold weather some wear fingerless gloves, though the *grade* will have to be lowered.

Gneiss. A beautiful, metamorphic rock, often containing banding. Can provide excellent climbing with good friction, though some small flakes can be suspect.

Gore-tex fabric. Nylon fabric which allows water vapour, eg, from perspiration, to pass through to the outside, while retaining a barrier to water, eg, rain. There are other fabrics and treatments of fabrics which act in a similar fashion to Gore-tex (patented by DuPont Chemicals), all working to some extent to provide a waterproof outer layer of clothing while allowing some degree of breathable comfort. These include: Sympatex, which is a laminate, and Entrant and Cyclone, both coatings. In general, a laminate will probably be more robust than a coating, particularly if a garment has many seams and stitching. In moist conditions, and with exercise, water vapour will still condense on the inner surface of an anorak, though the garment will remain much more comfortable to wear in wet conditions than a non-permeable nylon. The traditional, wax-impregnated cotton jackets work at least as well, though they are disadvantaged by heavier weight and a less hard-wearing fabric. Overtrousers, *bivouac bags*, boot liners, boots, gloves, all have been manufactured using Gore-tex.

Bivouac bags in particular gain much by being breathable.

In Gore-tex, the fabric, which is in the form of a sandwich of the actual Gore-tex with two outer layers of nylon, works by the fact that the pore size is such that smaller particles of water vapour can pass through, while relatively large water drops are prevented from entering. Obviously, the limit to efficiency is the rate at which water vapour can pass through. This will be affected by the amount of water vapour produced, and the differential between the inside and the outside humidities.

Grading. The classification of a climb according to its difficulty, permitting a climber to select a route commensurate with ability. Gradings have evolved with the sport, and in summer take into account both the technical difficulty of each pitch, the grade being that of the hardest move or moves, and the overall difficulty of the route, which could include its protection, strenuousness and so on. This double system of grading a rock climb (at least in Britain and in the Alps) indicates more about the route. For example, a route graded HVS, 5a will probably be well-protected, with its major technical difficulties relatively shortlived, whereas a route graded E2, 5b probably has prolonged and serious difficulties.

For rock climbs, various countries have devised different grading systems, shown in table form below. The comparisons are approximate only. Even moving between different areas and rock types in Britain the climber will experience some overlapping of the grades, though hopefully never to excess. A technical grade is really only valid for climbs of about Severe and upward. For winter climbs, much of the climbing world uses the Scottish system, ranging from Grade I, the easiest, to Grade VI. A comparison between this and the Continental, or UIAA (Union Internationale des Associations Alpines) system, is also given in the table. In Britain, as in other countries, the system is open ended, so that the next advance in technical standards can create a harder grade. At present, the hardest grade is E8, no doubt soon to be supplanted by an E9. At the harder end of the scale there is insufficient consensus of opinion to compare the different grading systems. **Tip**. When first climbing in a new area or crag, pick a route at least one full grade below your considered best for the day.

Winter Grades

The Scottish system, first developed in the Cairngorms, has found a fairly wide acceptance. It ranges from the easiest, I, to VI, with general conditions for each grade as described below:

I Simple snow slopes or gullies, with perhaps a small ice step or an easy cornice exit. Also includes straightforward ridges in good conditions.

II Snow gullies with a few short pitches. Exposed ridges with rocky sections.

III Multi-pitch gullies with long or difficult pitches equating approximately to Very Difficult in summer. The easier icefalls and buttresses.

IV Major gullies with several difficult pitches. Steeper icefalls and difficult buttresses. Sections of vertical or near-vertical ice.

V Major gullies with more continuous and steeper difficulties. Sections of vertical ice and long run-outs. Very difficult buttresses with technical mixed sections and/or long, exposed and serious run-outs.

VI Very steep and technical climbs,

British		UIAA	USA	Australia
Easy		I		
Moderate		II	5.0	4
Difficult		III −	5.1	5
		III	5.2	6
Very Difficult		III +	5.3	7
		IV	5.4	8, 9
Severe	4a, b	IV +	5.5	10, 11
		V	5.6	12, 13
			5.7	14
Very Severe	4c	V +	5.8	15
Hard Very Severe	5a	VI	5.9	16, 17
E1	5b	VI +	5.10a	18, 19
		VII −	5.10b	20
E2	5c	VII	5.10c	21
		VII +	5.10d	22
E3	6a	VIII −	5.11a	23
		VIII	5.11b	24
E4	6a, b	IX −	5.11c	25
		IX	5.12	26, 27
E5	6b, c			

usually of a mixed nature. Vertical and perhaps overhanging pitches and/or poor protection.

Sometimes a route may be given a split grade, e.g. III/IV.

Scottish/French equivalents are given below, from D (*Difficile*), to ED+ (*Extrêmement Difficile*).

Finally, routes climbed mainly with aid have their own grading system: from the easiest, A1, to A4, depending on such factors as the quality of the aid points, the difficulty in moving from one aid point to the next, and perhaps the quality of the rock.

Granite. A deep-formed, volcanic rock, with a crystalline structure and coarse grain. Much of the world's best climbing is on granite, which can form superb pillars, faces and slabs. The climbing is often strenuous, with cracks and blank sections of wall a typical feature. The Cairngorm Mountains in Scotland, Cornwall in England, the Poisoned Glen in

Scottish	I	II	III	IV	V	VI
French			D D+	TD− TD+	TD+ ED−	ED ED+

Ireland are all granite, as are the French Alps.

Gritstone. A sedimentary rock allied to sandstone but with rougher particles of quartz embedded in a matrix along with feldspar. There are many relatively short crags and outcrops of this rock, whose geological name is Millstone Grit, particularly in North and Central England. Its typically steep walls, combined with a dearth of incut holds, provides good, hard climbing, with strenuous overhangs and jam cracks a common feature.

Groove. A rock feature; an open fault intermediate in size between a crack and a chimney, and often more shallow than either.

Guidebooks. Often shortened to guides. Most climbing areas, unless newly discovered, will have their climbs described in a climbers' book or guide. A well-written guide will also describe access, history, local features and/or peculiarities of the area. The necessary map will be indicated. Route information will include the grade, both overall and technical if in the higher grades, the length, and quality, and also details of the first ascent. Responsibility for collation of information and publishing of guidebooks at appropriate intervals is commonly taken up by the large and sometimes national clubs; eg, in Britain we find The Fell & Rock C.C. for the Lake District, the Climbers Club for Wales, the Scottish Mountaineering Club for Scotland and so on. The writer or writers will be local experts and active climbers themselves.

There is, inevitably, a wide range of guidebook styles. Most climbing guides are now produced in a size suitable for fitting into a pocket as well as being bound in a plastic cover for protection from the elements.

Illustrations of crags accompanying route descriptions may use photographs or line drawings, with the latter usually the better. Some guidebooks also incorporate action photographs. These whet the appetite and indicate the nature of an area's climbing, especially when cloud obscures the real thing.

Guides. Professional climbers who make their living by, and can be hired for, climbing. Many will also instruct on courses, both summer and winter. There are recognized qualifications in many countries, with an exam system on top of the necessary experience and competence. Potential clients should ensure that their guide is qualified through such a system. Normally a guide will begin by earning a summer certificate, then progress to a winter certificate. Examinations are held at the national outdoor centres, eg, Glenmore Lodge, Aviemore, in Scotland, and Plas-y-Brenin, Wales. Details of courses and examinations can be had from the BMC (British Mountaineering Council).

Gully. A deep chasm between two rock buttresses or a similar fault running up a hillside. Some gullies provide good summer routes, though most are at their best in winter, as they are often formed by the erosion of weaker or shattered rock.

Hammer. Climbing tool designed to drive in rock pegs or ice screws. Now rarely carried by climbers in Britain, as improved *protection* equipment makes the use of pegs for protection virtually redundant. The peg hammer, as it is called, has a standard hammer head at one side, with a short spike at the other, useful for cleaning out cracks etc. It is conveniently carried in a *holster* and is

Harness

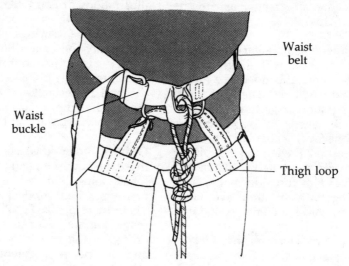

Waist belt

Waist buckle

Thigh loop

There are many designs of climbing harness. Some are integrated harnesses incorporating a pelvic and chest harness, favoured by some Alpine climbers. Most are as shown here, supporting the pelvic girdle only.

1. The Pat Littlejohn Harness, illustrated here, is a one-size harness, with adjustable leg loops allowing a comfortable and secure fit. The two thigh loops are joined to the waist loop by a figure-of-eight knot, finished with a double stopper knot. A karabiner is not required with this design of harness. Note that as with all harnesses using a buckle to fasten the waist belt, the strap should be fastened as for a normal buckle then followed back through the buckle again to prevent gradual slippage. Follow the manufacturer's instructions carefully for all harnesses.

best attached to the *harness* by a length of accessory cord. In winter it has been replaced by the *ice hammer*.

Hammock. Lightweight nylon net used for sleeping on steep routes with few convenient ledges, eg, the overhanging wall climbing of Yosemite in California. More recently, lightweight tents have been designed which can also be hung from a few aid points, such as the bat tent. Such tents require a floor held reasonably flat by a light alloy framework.

Hand traverse. To climb across a rock face relying mainly on hand holds. Normally of short duration only, and often strenuous. Some help can often be had from the feet by 'smearing', the friction obtained from sticky boot

soles placed flat on the rock.

Harness. A system of nylon integral waist and leg loops to which the main climbing ropes are attached. In the event of a fall, the load will be distributed around the climber's pelvic girdle, loading the bony areas and lessening the chances of damaging internal organs. Early harnesses on the Continent were of the chest or whole body type, and these are still used. British climbers favour the sit harness, of which the design by the late Don Whillans, the Whillans harness is perhaps best known. A disadvantage of the sit harness is that in a fall it is quite easy to end up hanging head down. This is avoided in the chest or body harnesses, which are however more restricting.

It is important to use the correct size of harness, and follow the maker's instructions carefully. Harnesses also have integral loops attached to the waist section for hanging gear from. In winter one or two hammer *holsters* can also be attached, for parking axes when not in use. Before harnesses were available the waist loop was often used, 6m of hemp cord wound round the waist and tied off with a *reef knot*. Hanging after a fall could lead to slow asphyxiation, with the diaphragm being compressed by the waist loop. These were replaced by waist belts, padded for comfort but still capable of allowing injury in a bad fall. American climbers often made a simple sit harness using nylon *tape* slings, known as a swami belt. These are all now redundant.

Hawser laid. The older method of rope construction, where the fibres are twisted into three or four strands which are then twisted into the rope.

This type of rope is weaker than *kernmantel* rope, twists badly under load, kinks more readily, while braking devices such as the *belay plate* are less effective. Superseded by *kernmantel* ropes in 1953.

Head torch. Battery-powered light worn round a climber's head or helmet. A necessary part of mountaineering equipment, especially in winter, with short daylight hours and possibility of benightment. In the Alps they permit night climbing or pre-dawn starts. Until very recently, most designs were atrocious, with climbers forced to modify existing models or make their own battery cases. Good modern designs, at present exemplified by the Petzl make, should incorporate features such as: broad elasticated strap for comfortable wearing round the head, focusing beam for different conditions, foolproof switching, so as to avoid accidental turning on in a rucksack, provision for storage of spare

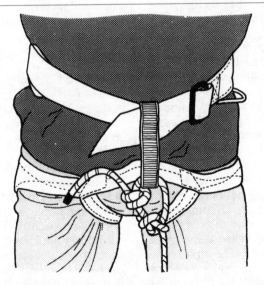

Harness

2. *A Camp harness, tied off using a bowline knot and a double stopper. Most harnesses, as this one, have loops to which protection gear can be attached.*

Head torch

Battery compartment

Spare bulbs
kept here

Focus
and on-off
ring

Safety catch

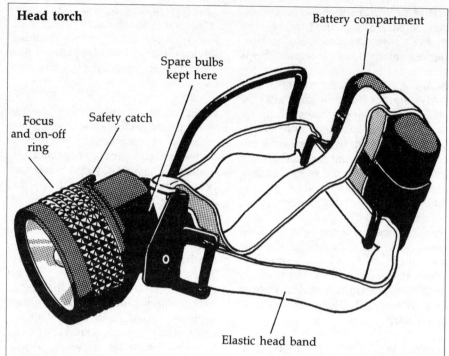

Elastic head band

A Petzl Zoom headtorch showing its salient features; elastic headband, battery container, focus and on-off ring.

bulbs. As yet, the initial cost and relatively short cycle life of rechargeable cells has kept their use down. Climbing *helmets* have buckles or shock cord attachment points front and back, for the head band of a head torch to be securely fixed.

Helicopter. Unless fortunate enough to be involved in some filming escapade, most climbers' experience of a helicopter will be through mountain rescue, probably involving the RAF Search and Rescue service. If an accident on a mountain has been notified to the police, and if circumstances warrant it, a helicopter may be called in. Daylight and reasonably good weather will usually be necessary, including clear visibility. If a victim has fallen on a cliff it will often be impossible to reach him or her directly. More often, a helicopter will

drop some members of the local rescue team with equipment, including a stretcher, so that the victim can be moved to a pick-up point. A helicopter, particularly a large one, requires upwards of 25m of obstruction-free ground to land safely. Much can be done by winch, particularly if the accident victim is not badly hurt.

If not directly involved with a rescue, keep out of the way. This applies even more to helicopter work, where there is a risk of injury from fast moving and invisible rotor blades. The helicopter likes to land into the wind, and may drop a smoke canister before approaching closely. If your position is not clearly known to the pilot, make it easy by being highly visible. Secure any loose equipment as there will be a strong downdraught from the rotors. Stay by the victim to protect from flying debris etc. The recognized signal by ground personnel needing help is to stand facing the helicopter with arms upraised in a V-shape. The signal that no help is required is to bring one arm down so that both arms are angled away from the body like a plane in a steep turn. Watch the pilot for any signals. If asked to approach a helicopter do so from the front. Stay away from both the tail rotor and the air intake, both of which are bad for health.

Helmet. Protective headgear worn by mountaineers. The existing choice of design is usually between a lighter Alpine-weight helmet of PBS plastic, or a heavier fibreglass model. The latter often curve down at the sides, giving more protection to the vulnerable areas round the ears and back of the skull. Helmets should have points for attaching a *head torch*. Most accidents in the hills involve head injuries. Having said that, many rock climbers do not now wear one. They are probably more necesssary, paradoxically, on the easier-angled routes, where a fall will mean hitting the slope instead of hanging in space. They are also more useful in winter, where there is a risk from falling lumps of ice. They should be worn for all Alpine routes, where there is a greater risk of falling rocks, ice etc. Unfortunately, hill-walkers are just as much at risk of head injury in a fall, though unlikely to wear helmets. Choose a size which is fairly snug but can still allow a balaclava to be worn. Helmets have an adjustable cradle allowing a little adjustment to be made.

Hemp rope. The rope in use for climbing until replaced by nylon during the Second World War. Among its many disadvantages were high weight, low breaking strength, poor handling. The usual method of construction was *hawser laid*, with Italian

Helicopter

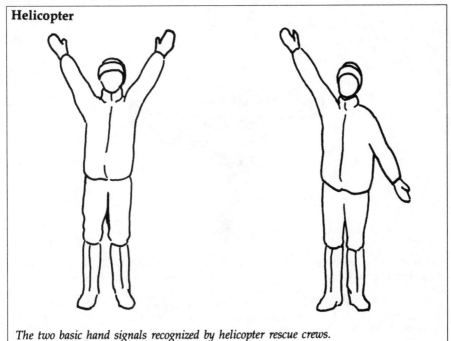

The two basic hand signals recognized by helicopter rescue crews.

Helmet

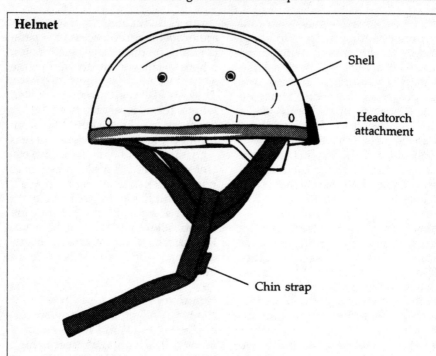

Shell

Headtorch attachment

Chin strap

1. A fairly light-weight climbing helmet, this one made by Viking in fibreglass.

2. The Pinnacle Climber helmet by Ultimate. The brim in this model descends slightly over the ears and back of the skull, providing extra protection. It has a polythene lining.

Other materials used for helmets include plastic, giving a lightweight Alpine-style helmet (e.g. Camp), and a fairly new Kevlar/Carbon glass fibre mix (e.g. the SM Kevlar Carbon).

hemp commonly used. The rationale that 'the leader must not fall' stems from the fact that the hemp rope would probably have snapped, even if the belay had held. The first ascent of the Matterhorn for example, in 1865, was made using an Alpine Club rope of white Manila hemp, with a diameter of 12mm and an approximate static breaking strength of 730kg. Even if in perfect condition, this rope would probably be unable to hold a fall of 10m by a leader weighing 80kg. This knowledge gave rise to the *dynamic belay*, where an experienced second with a good belay (and hopefully wearing gloves), would attempt to allow some rope to pass through the belay system, thereby spreading the loading and minimizing the chance of a rope failure. This was obviously a hit or miss affair, no matter how skilled the climbers.

Hero loop. See *extenders*.

Hexentric. See *chockstones*.

High altitude. Mountaineering at an altitude of over about 6000m, and therefore necessarily confined to the high mountain ranges of the world eg, the Himalaya, Andes, Alaska etc. In addition to the problems facing an expedition, there exist the difficulties posed by physiological changes. Though individuals differ, most climbers living at altitudes of 6000m plus are slowly deteriorating physically, and consequently have a limit on the time they can spend at altitude. This partly explains the need to descend to lower camps for rests while on a major expedition. Reduced oxygen at altitude makes any work hard and sleeping is also disrupted. For reasons not entirely clear, pulmonary or cerebral oedema is an associated risk, particularly in younger climbers. The only cure is an immediate descent to lower altitudes. Equipment must be of the very best, as temperatures and winds at high altitudes will be a severe test. A major expedition will carry oxygen cylinders and breathing apparatus. While the trend has been to climb at altitude without breathing oxygen, it may be required for sleeping and medicinal purposes.

Hill walking. The ascent of hills for pleasure, normally with little or no technical climbing necessary. Basic equipment includes the same *clothing* as for climbing, as well as a map and *compass*, *headtorch*, perhaps *bivouac* gear, spare food and clothing. In winter, in addition to the above, an *ice axe* and *crampons* should be carried. The emphasis for safe hill walking is on good navigation and a reasonable degree of fitness. In Scotland, the hill walking/climbing of *Munros*, distinct mountains of 3,000 ft or over, is a popular pastime.

Hold. An irregularity of rock which can be used by a climber for progress or rest. May come in any shape or form, from cracks, ripples, crystals, *flakes*, *spikes* etc. Small holds can be used by the finger tips only, while larger ones may be grasped by the whole hand. In winter climbing, hand or foot holds may be cut in snow or ice by an *axe*. The more difficult the rock climbing encountered, the more subtle the use of holds. Many holds, for example, may be used in one direction only, perhaps from the side, while others may be used to push upon, and not pull on. *Pinch grip* holds come into use increasingly in harder climbing, and are similar to the way one removes a book from a shelf. Large holds are often pushed down on, especially when attempting a *mantel-*

shelf move. The edge of a crack may be used as a *layback*, while a suitable crack can be *jammed*.

Holster. Conical, plastic attachment worn on a *harness* to hold an *axe* or *ice hammer*. Many winter climbers have two.

Huts. Many mountainous countries have climbing huts placed at strategic sites. These huts vary from the spartan one-room with a concrete floor to multi-storey buildings of relative luxury. Most are owned and/or run by mountaineering clubs or national bodies. In Europe many huts have a resident warden or guardian, who may, for an extra charge, provide meals or cook climbers' food. In Britain most huts do not have a resident warden, and have to be booked in advance, usually through one's club. Many clubs have reciprocal rights, which may make it easier and slightly cheaper to obtain bookings. See *bothies*.

Hypothermia. See *exposure*.

Ice axe. Winter climbing tool designed for walking and climbing over snow and ice. Used for balance, *step cutting*, and *front pointing*. The basic design has not changed much since the mid-eighteenth century, the axe having a head end with pick and adze, a shaft of varying length depending on the function of the axe, and a lower end tapering to a spike. There will normally be a drilled hole through the head or shaft, and perhaps one through the top of the spike, both allowing a sling or length of accessory cord to be attached. Originally, axes had wooden shafts of ash or hickory, now mostly replaced by lightweight alloys of far greater strength. The metal shaft is usually covered with a rubber sleeve, provid-

Ice axe

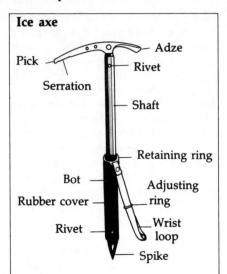

1. *A standard, metal-shafted walking/easy climbing ice axe. The length of this model, the Stubai Yellow Star, is 63 cm, about average length for a general purpose axe.*
  The wrist loop is attached to the shaft by a sliding retaining ring, so that the axe may be used for cutting steps or for walking, with the hand holding the axe (see next illustration). A bolt prevents the wrist loop from sliding all the way down the shaft (it may be removed). The wrist loop itself can be adjusted by means of a sliding ring. The rubber cover on the shaft gives a well-insulated and secure grip.

ing insulation and a better grip.
  For walking, the length of the axe is dependent on the user's height, the spike being just short of the floor when held by the head and hung alongside the leg. Its length can vary from about 55cm to 90cm. A walking axe need not be made to as high a specification as a climbing axe, as its sole purpose is usually as an aid to balancing, step cutting, and *braking* during a fall. Its pick will not be extremely curved or bent down, as it will not be used for front pointing. The use of a sling on a walking axe depends on the owner's preference. It can prevent acute embarrassment if an axe is accidentally dropped,

Ice axe

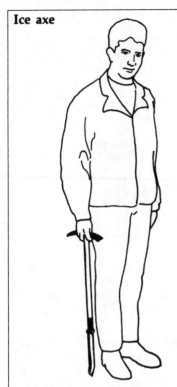

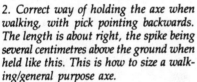

2. Correct way of holding the axe when walking, with pick pointing backwards. The length is about right, the spike being several centimetres above the ground when held like this. This is how to size a walking/general purpose axe.

3. Holding the axe when walking, with wrist loop in use. The sliding retaining ring is at the top of the shaft, with the wrist loop tightened so that the axe will not be lost if dropped.

though it can be a nuisance if the holding hand has to be changed frequently.

A useful way of storing the axe if both hands need to be used, eg, for a short scramble, is to push it down between the rucksack and one's back, placing it diagonally so that its head lies across one of the shoulder straps of the rucksack, which prevents it from slipping down, and its spike sticks out to one side. It can then be quickly pulled out if needed. Be sure to remember to remove the axe before removing the rucksack however, otherwise the axe will be dropped. Covers for both the head and spike are obtainable for travel or storage.

These can prevent personal injury from a sharp pick or spike if carrying it in a public place.

The climbing axe is shorter, varying from 45cm to 65cm in length, and may be built to higher specifications as it is more likely to have the weight of a climber utterly dependent on it. There is a choice of design of head, with two basic styles: the curved pick, and the angled pick. These new designs came about in the latter half of the 1960s, when Yvon Chouinard in the States and Hamish MacInnes in Scotland worked out two answers to the same question — how to design a pick which would hold a climber's weight and not slip out

Ice axe

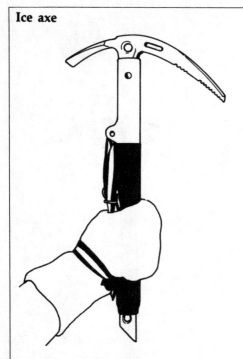

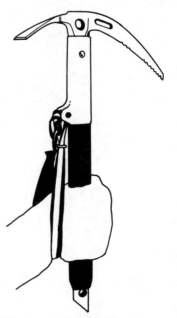

4. A front-pointing axe, the Stubai Sierra, being held using a wrist loop. Although this way of inserting the hand through the loop, with the loop between thumb and the rest of the hand, is the mechanically efficient way, the wrist loop lying along the shaft, most climbers seem to hold it as in the next illustration.

5. With the wrist loop used in this way, there is a higher probability of the hand slipping out of the loop in a fall, in addition to which the loop is angled away from the shaft, which immediately places the system at a mechanical disadvantage. It may be slightly easier, however, to hang from the loops using this method, though it is important to have sufficiently tight loops.

when picked into snow or ice. Chouinard opted for a curved pick, MacInnes for a steeply angled pick. Since then, a variation on the inclined pick has emerged, the banana pick, which has a pick inclined down them curving slightly up. All work well enough and the choice is largely a personal one, though recent use suggests a bias towards the banana. The head, whatever its shape, is made of high quality steel with some trace elements thrown in for complex metallurgical reasons. As different designs and lengths of axe will have different 'feels', it helps to handle one before deciding, preferably on a route using a borrowed tool.

When front pointing started, short axes were the favoured style, taken to extremes perhaps with the Terrordactyl designed by MacInnes. These worked very well, but had the disadvantage of a short reach, a handicap for icy bulges. The other handicap was the small clearance between pick and shaft due to the steep angle on the pick. This led to 'Terrordactyl knuckle', with bruised knuckles due to climbers striking the ice. The lower edge of the pick has a number of serrations, designed to steady the axe on penetration. One disadvantage is that they can catch when withdrawal is attempted, leading to a desperate

Ice axe

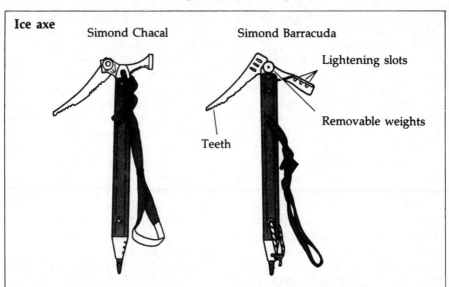

Simond Chacal   Simond Barracuda

Lightening slots

Removable weights

Teeth

6. *Two modern classic front-pointing axes — the Simond Chacal and Barracuda. These are very well made banana pick axes, the picks of both tools curving slightly upwards towards the extremities. The adze tool, the Barracuda, in this illustration has a small loop of accessory cord tied through the bottom hole, just above the spike. This could be used to clip into the harness in a steep position, for a rest or belay.*

The Barracuda, in common with several other makes, has a variable weight system, allowing four, two or no metal disks to be attached to the head, according to the user's preference. The teeth have been partially filed down, to facilitate easy removal.

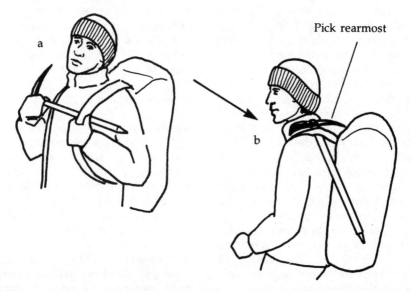

a

Pick rearmost

b

7. *Temporary storage of ice axe between shoulder and rucksack. This is a convenient way of stashing away the axe, perhaps in order to use both hands to scramble. Remember to remove the axe before taking the sack off, however!*

struggle by a climber trying to free the axe. Many manufacturers cut too many of these teeth, particularly on the Simond range. **Tip**. File the teeth down to about half their original depth. The pick will work as well but stick much less often. Use a hand file and vice and be patient — the metal is tough! Many adzes will have slots cut through to lighten the weight.

The shaft is a flattened oval in cross section, the best shape for gripping and accurate aim, while a rubber cover keeps it warm and easy to grip. There should be one or two holes through the shaft, allowing accessory cord to be tied for attachment to the *harness* and/or a sling for the wrist loop. The wrist loop is critical, as it may have to support the entire weight of its user. It will be attached to the hole through the axe head or near the top of the shaft. The size and length of the loop must be carefully gauged. The loop must be large enough so that a fully gloved hand can be inserted without too much of a struggle, but not so large that in a sudden slip the hand would come out, leaving the axe in the slope and the climber some distance below.

It may be necessary to support one's weight from one axe, by inserting one arm through the loop as far as the elbow, especially when inserting an *ice screw*, so allow for this. A commercially made wrist loop should have an adjusting device, such as a sliding band, allowing the wrist loop to be narrowed or widened according to needs. For climbing, the inserted hand should end up grasping the shaft just above the start of the spike, so as to use the full length of the axe. The attachment holes are usually only large enough to allow 15mm tape to be used for the wrist loop.

Some climbers have rubber cords holding down the wrist loop on the shaft, thereby maintaining the direction of pull close to the axis of the shaft and hopefully keeping the pick in the ice. This can be a nuisance, particularly when climbing mixed ground, as the axe will dangle awkwardly when released to use a rock hold. A sling may be used to connect the axes to the harness. There should be a hole near the spike for this purpose: if not use one higher up the shaft. Some climbers do not use these slings, relying on good wrist loops and confidence not to drop the axe. If using them, have them long enough so as not to impede a high upward stretch for a placement. Slings are irritating in use, but can be be very useful for supplementary belays, rests etc. Perhaps a good compromise is to have small loops in place which can then be easily connected to the harness when needed. Check wrist loops and slings regularly for wear and tear, and axe heads for any loosening of rivets etc. There is little to be gained by sharpening picks: a mild going over with a file to remove burrs once or twice a season is good enough, any more and the pick will wear down quickly and may even bend in use.

Ice climbing. See *front pointing*.

Icefall. On a large scale, the area of a glacier where a steepening causes the flowing ice to break into crevasses, pinnacles, and dangerously unstable cliffs. The pinnacles are also known as séracs. On a smaller scale, ice pitches on a cliff are frequently referred to as icefalls.

Ice hammer. Climbing tool designed for winter climbing, with a hammer head replacing the adze. Normally used in conjunction with an *ice axe* for *front pointing*. The hammer is slightly heavier than the axe, to facilitate the

Ice screw

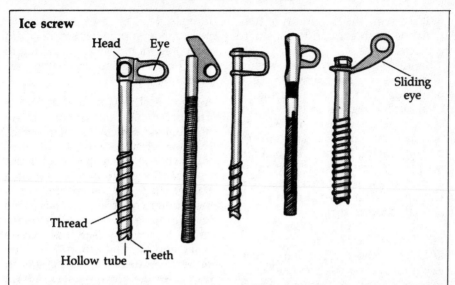

Head   Eye

Sliding
eye

Thread

Hollow tube   Teeth

1. Various models of tubular ice screws. The model on the far right has a sliding eye. When at the head end of the screw it can be used as a ratchet to screw or unscrew the ice screw. If the screw is not fully home, it can be slid down until resting on the surface of the ice, thus reducing the leverage.

2. A drive in, known as a Warthog due to the ribs or spirals. It is hammered in and screwed out, its tapered shape making it easier to place.

placing of pegs and *ice screws*. Some designs have removable weights, to allow the balance and weight to be tailored to a climber's personal preference. These are usually secured by a bolt, using a key supplied with the hammer.

Ice screw. Metal device for belaying or protection on hard snow, ice, or frozen turf. Original designs were similar to corkscrews and, due to their intrinsic weakness, were best confined to opening wine bottles. Later models were tubular, with a thread running on the outside of the tube. A second design in use is the *drive in*, a solid screw thinner than the tubular and tapering towards the point. It is best to carry both when ice climbing, as both have their uses. The drive in is quickly hammered in and slowly screwed out. As it is thinner than a tubular ice screw its holding power is less, perhaps 700kg at best. It has the virtue of being placed quickly, with the minimum of fuss, which is often enough to safeguard a crucial move.

Before placing any screw ensure that loose surface snow or ice is removed. Place a screw at an angle of about 80 degrees to the ice; this should ensure that it will be optimally placed to avoid an outward pull. If placing in water ice bad *dinner plating* may make it difficult or even impossible to use a screw. **Tip**. Hammer in the drive in then give it a final quarter turn to bed in its 'warts' or projecting bumps. Do not tie off a partly embedded drive in, as its holding power will be dangerously low (unless of course you have nothing else!). To remove either a drive in or tubular, insert the pick of an axe through the eye and use the extra leverage so obtained to easily turn the screw.

To insert a tubular screw a few taps with a pick will prepare the target spot on the snow or ice. A gentle tap on the screw will then help it on its way. The first few turns may be done by hand, using the eye as leverage; thereafter insert the axe pick through the eye of the screw and rotate until fully embedded. If the screw has bottomed, due to an inadequate thickness of ice, either select an alternative spot or tie off the screw using a *clove hitch* on a sling. Remove the screw by the reverse process. The tubular screw, due to its greater diameter, has a greater holding power than the drive in, perhaps upwards of 1200kg in good ice. Salewa, Chouinard, DMM, Cassin and others, all manufacture good quality screws. Some are made with Continental ice in mind, something which should be kept in mind if buying for the generally thinner British variety.

For main belays screws should be placed in pairs: at least a metre apart

if possible. The axes can also be picked in as supplementary belays in steep situations, being connected to the belay system by slings as necessary.

Insurance. The United Kingdom is unusual in that mountain rescues are not charged directly to the rescued. Even so, climbers wishing to cover increasingly expensive equipment from theft etc, often do so under a household policy. When climbing in most other countries, it is advisable to take out a specialized insurance cover, to pay for gear loss, rescue costs, and hospitalization. There are some allowances for Europeans in European countries — seek advice well in advance as it will probably be necessary to apply for forms in advance of going out. In Britain a climber should ask for an E111 form from the local DHSS office; it may help slightly if hospitalized. The BMC can advise on insurance, as well as sell cover.

International Distress Signal. A sequence of six regularly spaced signals, followed by a one-minute gap, then repeated. The signal may be by torch, whistle etc as appropriate. The reply is a sequence of three signals, again with one-minute gaps between.

Italian friction hitch. (USA — Munter hitch.) A knot for a single rope, useful for bringing up a second on a direct belay, for example on an easy winter climb. As it is similar in appearance to a *clove hitch*, it must be practised so as not to cause confusion. It can also be used in place of a *descender* for an abseil, in conjunction with a *screw gate karabiner*.

Jamming. A method of climbing cracks by inserting part of one's anatomy, commonly a hand, arm, or foot, then fixing the hand etc, in the crack

Italian friction hitch

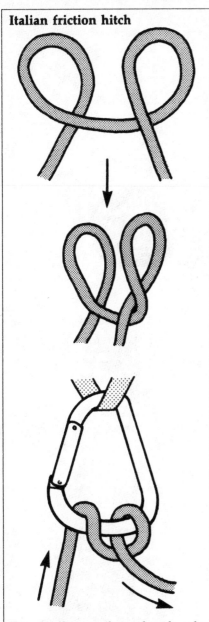

Form two loops as shown then close the two faces together like a book.

An excellent friction knot for use as a belay, or for abseiling in conjunction with a karabiner. When used as a belay to bring up a climber it has the versatility of being directionally reversible, switching at the pull of the rope.

so as to be able to rely on the jam for a pull, rest and so on. The fingers are the smallest units which can be jammed, followed by the hand, in a flattened profile at first then, as the cracks become wider, bunched into a fist. The best part of a crack to use for a jam is often just above a constriction, much as it would be for a *chockstone* runner. If a foot is used as a jam in a narrow crack, the toes may have to be inserted sideways with the ankle twisted upright. Jamming may be painful, though when performed by an expert some amazing cracks can be climbed with little apparent effort. If used regularly, eg, in some North American areas, it is advisable to tape the knuckles, which take much of the brunt. Jamming is a technique which needs to be experimented with, preferably on short, safe outcrop routes. Postgraduate students of jamming can try climbing an *off-width* crack, one too wide to jam, but too narrow to allow the entire body to enter. A strange and indefinable mixture of brute strength, cunning and something else seems to be required here, though many climbers have taken to avoiding them completely. (See drawings on pages 100-1.)

Jug handle. The ideal rock hold, being large enough for the whole hand to fit over, and often incut. It can support the entire body weight with the minimum of effort.

Jumar. A design of mechanical device used to climb a rope. There are several models available, usually in left and right hand pairs, of which the generic name has been taken from the original. Invented in the 1950s by a Swiss pair, Adolf **Jusi** and Walter **Marti**, to help in the banding of birds for the Swiss Government. The fundamental design incorporates

Jamming

1. *A tight jam for the left fist.*

2. *A middle-sized fist jam. If need be, this can support the entire body weight.*

3. *Close-up of 2. A middle-sized hand jam. Often the thumb will be placed on the palm of the hand, to increase the size of the fist, allowing bigger cracks to be jammed.*

a hinged metal arm which allows the jumar to be pushed up a rope, but which grips the rope firmly when loaded. The *prusik knot* mimics this action. The upper jumar, as with the prusik knot, is attached to the *harness*, while the lower jumar is attached to a foot loop. The climber then jumars up the rope by pushing the jumars up alternately. Jumars are extensively used in long *aid routes* and on *expeditions*, for protection on long sections of **fixed ropes**. See *ascenders*. (See drawings on page 102.)

Karabiner. Often shortened to 'krab'. An oval or D-shaped alloy ring, with a spring-loaded gate on one of the long sides. The Italian spelling is carabiner, used in the USA. The German spelling is with a 'k', as used here. Karabiners are used extensively in climbing for attachment of ropes, slings, runners etc. Basic design, the snaplink, has a simple gate; for attaching the main climbing rope to a harness and for other uses where security is vital, a *screw gate* or locking model may be used. In this, the gate has a collar which can be screwed over the end of the gate, preventing accidental opening. In practice, screw gates are unnecessary for *runners*, as it is very unusual for both the gate to be opened accidentally, and for the rope to be freed from the karabiner. The screw gate model has been taken one stage fur-

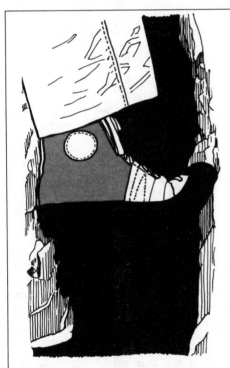

4. An off-width crack is often a good place for a foot jam. The heel and toe are on opposing walls of the crack, using friction and/or any small hold that can be found.

Jamming

5. As a crack becomes narrower, it will no longer be possible to use a hand jam. Instead, the fist is opened and the fingers are inserted, then bent so that they jam securely in the crack. If the crack is slightly wider than the one illustrated, the thumb may be palmed, slightly increasing the width of the jam.

Jumar

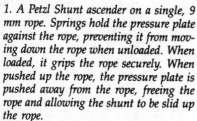

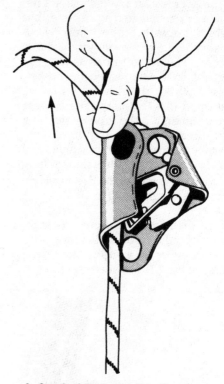

1. A Petzl Shunt ascender on a single, 9 mm rope. Springs hold the pressure plate against the rope, preventing it from moving down the rope when unloaded. When loaded, it grips the rope securely. When pushed up the rope, the pressure plate is pushed away from the rope, freeing the rope and allowing the shunt to be slid up the rope.

2. Standard Petzl Expedition basic ascender, in closed position on a single, 9mm rope.

ther, with a self-locking model. Experienced climbers find these irritating to use, but they probably have a place for instructional schools, where beginners cannot be relied upon to remember to close a screw gate. Large pear-shaped krabs with locking gates are useful when used with *belay plates* or with a double rope tied in an *Italian friction hitch*, as the ropes will run more smoothly.

The main requirements for a karabiner are that it be light, strong and easy to clip into a rope or runner with one hand. D-shaped krabs are stronger than ovals, as the D-shape puts more than half the load on the non-gate side of the krab. The strongest krabs have ratings of over 3000kg, while the lightest are about 1800kg and weigh about 40gm. It is probably better to stick to a minimum breaking strain of about 2100kg for the plain or 'vanilla' krabs, and about 2500kg minimum for the screw gates. The ultra-lightweight krabs have a use in climbing the very hard routes — where often the protection is not great in any case. No point combining a 3000kg krab with a 360kg micro nut. These figures are for a krab with closed gate, the strength goes down markedly if the gate is open, for example if the krab is pressing against a rock edge. Typically, the strength will reduce to a third or even a quarter of the gate-shut strength. Take care to prevent this situation, which though rare, can obviously happen. Avoid also placing a three-

Karabiner

Chouinard
2000 kg

Cassin
2250 kg

Clog
3000 kg

Clog
3000 kg
screwgate

1. Common types of
karabiners in use.

Cassin pear
2250 kg

DMM self-locking pear
2200 kg

2. An accident situation, with a too-short sling on a flake producing a three-way loading on a snaplink karabiner. Avoid this by using a longer sling or two slings joined together. The karabiner in this situation could withstand only a very small load and could easily open.

way loading on a krab, such as can happen if too short a sling is used for a flake runner or belay. The strength in this situation will also be markedly reduced, typically from 2200kg to about 650kg.

Recent testing on krabs, involving dropping them on to concrete surfaces from height, indicates that they can tolerate this outrage to a certain degree. More serious is climbing on a sea cliff, with the likelihood of corrosion from salt-laden air. Following a sea cliff outing wash them in fresh water to remove salts, which can otherwise quickly initiate an electrolytic reaction with the alloy. Likewise wash your grubby hands following a bout of fish-and-chips, as the acids and salts here can also affect your gear. **Tip**. Sticky gate action may be helped with a little silicone spray lubricant. Krabs may be identified with a piece of coloured tape conveniently wrapped round the long side, usually obscuring the maker's name or the marked strength of the krab, which proves that the manufacturers have got this aspect of design wrong.

Kernmantel. Contemporary method of rope construction, invented in 1953 by the German manufacturers Edelrid. The rope is constructed in two parts, with an internal core (Kern) surrounded and protected by a mantle (Mantel). The core is at least 50% of the total weight of the rope. The mantle is braided round the core and protects it against the constant abrasion the rope will receive during its working life. With a little use, the outer threads of the mantle will be pulled out into tiny loops and also frayed, to produce a 'furry' appearance to the rope. This increases the grip on the rope. It will also, with longer use and further abrasion, cause a rope to shorten by upwards

of 3–5% of its original length. The strength will be slightly reduced due to the same wear and tear, though not by any serious amount unless badly frayed by sharp edges, crampon points etc. The mantle is distinctively coloured so as to allow for easy visibility and to differentiate between ropes when climbing with double ropes. Edelrid have a colour coding which determines the year of manufacture.

The UIAA has a standard method of rope testing, involving dropping a weight in controlled circumstances. All climbing ropes should come under this scheme, and will be labelled as being acceptable. Rope used for leading will be *fall factor* rated, typically a minimum of three, having passed this dynamic test three or more times in succession without breaking. The weight used is 80kg, the length it falls is 5m, with a fall factor of 1.78. Edelrid 9mm rope, using a 55kg weight, is rated at 12–14 falls, with a static breaking strength of 1530kg. Beal 9mm ropes, with 1630kg strength, are rated at 13–15 falls. The design of a good climbing rope is a compromise between the rope having a low impact force — the amount of stress exerted on the rope during its first UIAA dynamic test — and the amount the rope stretches under load. The impact force is also proportional to the force driving the rope against a sharp edge, which we obviously wish to minimize. We do not want a rope which has too much strength under loading, as then a falling climber would easily fall too far and land on the ground, hence the compromise. Typically, a good rope will stretch anything from about 5–8% under body weight alone, about 50% in a bad fall. This elongation is designed to absorb the energy in a fall. Interestingly, the human body will absorb 10–15% of the energy of a fall, reducing the loading on other parts of the system.

Several factors will reduce the strength of a rope. Passing over a sharp edge will risk cutting the rope on loading, by a straightforward shearing effect. The strength is reduced by turning round a curve, eg, running through a karabiner of edge radius 5mm reduces the rope strength to about 70%. Avoid at all costs having a rope run over another rope or sling. The friction generated can easily burn through one of the ropes. When storing a climbing rope, keep it away from all chemicals. This includes car battery acid, which has fatally weakened at least one leader's rope. **Tip**. If the rope becomes dirty wash it in a washing machine, mild soap, warm water, no spinning. Hang the rope out to dry. This will remove small particles of grit etc which would hasten the wear of the rope. If you climb often in winter the sheath will be kept clean by the snow, though there may be hidden particles of grit.

The first rope bought by a beginner might usefully be a 45m length of 11mm. This will allow routes in the easier grades to be climbed, and rope and protection technique to be learned without the additional complexity of handling a *double rope*. Later on, a 45m length of 9mm rope, also known as a half-rope, can be bought, especially if by now some regular climbing partner has been found who can have the other rope, hopefully of a different colour! Some modern young climbers, trained on *climbing walls*, will no doubt go straight to 9mm ropes. A few experienced climbers use 50m lengths, useful in winter for longer runouts, though obviously that bit heavier. Check the ropes regularly for excess wear, avoid standing on them, take care in use by intelligent place-

ment of belays and protection, do not have big falls, and a rope used most weekends might be safe for about two years normal climbing. If badly worn, or if the recipient of a severe loading, then do not gamble, throw it out. **Tip**. If the colour of your rope has faded, so has its strength, as you have had it for too long.

The use of rope material called Kevlar is about to expand, and it may be that this new rope material will oust perlon for use with *chockstones*. Called Spectra or Blue Water in the UK, 5.5mm diameter rope made from this material is, at 2045kg, stronger than 8mm kernmantel and even stronger than 3.18mm steel cable. As Kevlar (courtesy of DuPont) is about 50% lighter than similarly sized perlon rope, is cut-resistant and has a high melting-point core, it seems, despite its greater cost, to be the material to consider when buying a new chockstone. When tied with a *double fisherman's knot* on a *hexentric*, the strength has been measured as 1590kg, considerably stronger, despite being smaller and lighter. It is also available as tape, with a 15mm *extender* having a quoted strength of 2700kg or 2200kg, depending on the extender.

To thread kernmantel accessory cords through chockstones, a tight fit may be accommodated by the following method. Gently melt one end of the cord without setting fire to it. Avoid the molten drips, which can burn. Using an old knife blade or spoon, shape the soft end into a tapered finish. Once cool, the tapered end can be pushed through one of the bottom holes in a chockstone, twisting strongly at the same time. Pull some slack through then repeat the process, going into the top of the other hole to emerge at the bottom. Adjust the positions of the two ends, and tie off with a double fisherman's knot, finishing by taping the ends with your choice of coloured adhesive tape. The method of threading a tape sling is similar. There is an important difference when it comes to finishing Kevlar cord, however. The core of this has a very high melting-point, so that only the sheath can be melted. First of all, use either a very sharp blade or wire cutters, and cut the cord so that the sheath can be pulled back, exposing about 1 cm of the core. Cut off the exposed core then pull the sheath back over the core. Melt the sheath, so that the soft ends can be pinched together. Finally, gently heat the end again so that it fuses into a solid, closed mass, enclosing the core completely.

An allowance for knots should be made when buying cord or tape for making up runners. Using a double fisherman's knot for accessory cord, the approximate lengths required for the knot with 5, 6, 7 or 8mm cord will be 35, 40, 45 and 50cm respectively. With tape, and using the *tape knot*, 15mm tape will require 45cm, and 25mm tape will require 55cm. Experiment with these measurements. So to estimate what length of sling you will need, decide on the finished (looped) length, double this, then

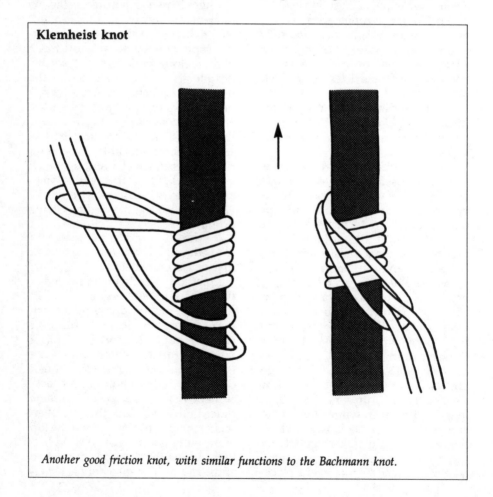

Klemheist knot

Another good friction knot, with similar functions to the Bachmann knot.

Layback

The hands pull while the feet push. Maintain fairly straight arms and move feet and hands up in small steps.

add the appropriate amount for the knot as given above.

Kevlar. See *kernmantel*.

Klemheist knot. A friction knot used for the same purposes as the *prusik knot*, eg, climbing a fixed rope, securing the main rope to a belay so as to escape the belay system etc. The amount of friction can be varied according to the number of turns given round the main rope. As with the prusik knot, a 6mm diameter accessory cord will work best on both 9 and 11mm ropes.

Knots. See the separate entries for each knot, which include; *Bachmann, bowline, clove hitch, double fisherman's,*

Italian friction hitch, Klemheist, overhand, Penberthy, prusik, reef, sheet bend, single fisherman's, stopper, tape, Tarbuck.

Layback. Rock climbing technique useful for cracks, flakes and steep edges. Often strenuous, it involves opposing forces, the hands usually pulling while the feet are pushing. To reduce the work, maintain fairly straight arms, and of course use any foothold that turns up. A long layback can be serious, as it is often very difficult to place protection, both hands being needed. The feet are often used on friction holds only, while the hands may have to be shuffled up the rock or moved up in small steps only. Some climbs require a similar technique for a move or two only, when they are called a layaway move, typically when using a handhold which is only good for a sidepull. A good technique to practise using a top rope on a local crag or climbing wall.

Leader. The first climber on a rope, who is moving up while belayed by the *second*. A rope of two equally talented climbers usually make alternate leads, though sometimes one leader will dominate and will do all or most of the leading on a climb. The consequences of a fall for the leader are naturally more serious than for a second, who will have the security of a rope from above, so that boldness is a typical characteristic of a good leader. It is rewarding to lead, finding the route, placing the protection, making the decisions. A good second, however, should not be overlooked. The second has to maintain the free-running of the ropes, be aware of potential hazards for the leader, and provide a sensible blend of encouragement and caution. Some climbers are content to second, some have to lead.

Leading through. Two climbers on a multi-pitch route making alternate leads. If the climbers are of fairly equal skill this saves time, as the belay does not have to be changed at the start of every pitch. On long and difficult Alpine routes, some climbers lead a number of pitches in succession, before handing over the lead to their companion. This provides the second with some sort of a rest from the physical and mental stress associated with leading.

Ledge. A flat section on an otherwise inclined mountain face. May vary from a few centimetres to many metres wide, and can be of any length. Provides a natural belay stance and also a potential bivouac spot on a multi-day route. Some ledges have been used for *girdle traverses*.

Lightning. A weather hazard on mountains, particularly in the Alps. The electrical discharge between ground and cloud of different potential will often strike on isolated, high features, eg, summits, pinnacles, ridges, arêtes. In a thunderstorm, or where a thunderstorm seems to be building up, avoid such features. Avoid also gullies, wide cracks and similar features on a mountain, as lightning is often channelled into these. Lightning is often preceded by an increase in static, with warning signs such as hair rising and ice axes hissing. It will probably be unwise to cross exposed, open ground while a thunderstorm is happening, just as it is unwise to take shelter under a tree which can attract a lightning strike. The safe area to be during an electrical storm, if you have a choice, is on open ground at least 3m away from a rock wall, and not under a boulder. Sit on something dry, such as a rope or rucksack, and minimize the contact area with the ground.

Limestone. A sedimentary rock of marine origin, often containing fossil remains. Limestone crags are frequently steep and smooth, therefore providing much hard rock climbing of a strenuous, fingery nature. Many of the limestone crags in Britain, indeed, were of interest to *aid climbers* for the most part, though many of the old aid routes are now climbed free. Old river gorges provide much of the limestone climbing, while the Dolomites in Italy have remarkable towered peaks providing many steep, hard routes.

Line. a) The way taken by a route, and followed by climbers. A good line may be one which follows some strong, natural weakness up the mountain, eg, a line of cracks, or a gully.
b) Obsolescent term for small diameter *hawser-laid rope* used for *abseils, prusik loops* etc. Now replaced by *accessory cord*.

Lip salve. A cream used for protection from the sun, especially on *glaciers* and at *high altitude*. Prevents the lips from drying out and becoming painfully cracked.

Loose rock. Not all rock is firm and secure. Part of every good climber's stock of skills is handling loose rock on a climb. The first state is to recognize loose rock. Often it will be obvious by its appearance alone. Unless absolutely necessary, do not use loose rock for holds, runners etc. Ensure that the ropes will not run over loose rock in such a way as to knock it down. Occasionally, a leader may be able to remove loose rock from a climb and safely throw it down. Only do this if the rock is a potential hazard to climbers and if it is safe to do so, with no one below and the total certainty that no one is hidden below either. In some cases it may be possible to leave the loose rock for the second to deal with. There will often be some loose rock on a *first ascent*.

If a hold is suspected of being loose it can often be tested by thumping it with a fist. A hollow sound announces its false heart. Whether you then use it depends on your need, the degree of looseness etc. Minimize the force exerted on it if you have to use it. Most dangerous of all are holds which look sound, test out alright, then fail when used. Fortunately this does not happen too often. Certain types of rock may have this unsettling behaviour more often than others, particularly the crystalline, metamorphic rocks such as the schists and quartzites found in Scotland. Thin flakes, quartz ripples, all of these should be suspect.

Lowering. There are several occasions during climbing when it may be necessary to lower a climber down a face using rope. A leader may fail at a hard section and retreat or fall off. The second then has the task of lowering the deposed climber from a runner, usually the highest one, unless it is of dubious worth, in which case the leader may try to reach the next runner by down climbing or attempt to put in a more secure runner. There should be little difficulty in lowering a leader from a good runner using a *belay brake* or *Italian hitch*, as there will be a great deal of friction in the system. The lowered climber may have a choice between leaving the ropes clipped into runners as the retreat continues, or removing the protection on the descent, depending on the circumstances.

It is also necessary, on occasion, to lower a second. Perhaps an inexperienced second has become tired and requires lowering to a convenient resting point below the hard move. Providing the belay is good, there is a belay brake of some kind and the belayer is in a good position to be braced, there should be little problem, particularly if the second can take some of the weight off the rope by using hands and feet. A problem might arise if the ground is steep, the stance poor, and the belayer has been pulled off. Provided panic has not set in however, the brake will have worked, the harness will be taking much of the punishment, and the lower will not go on for ever. It may be necessary, in order to go to the rescue of a partner, to escape the belay system. See *belay*.

Mantelshelf. Climbing move required to gain a high ledge or hold. The hands are placed on the hold or ledge and the arms straightened, the body being pulled up high enough so that a foot can be placed on the ledge beside a hand. At this point, if in balance on the ledge, the other foot can be brought on to the ledge as well, otherwise a handhold may have to be sought on the rock above. This move is often required to be made when intermediate footholds are missing, or when moving over a bulge or overhang. (See drawings on pages 110-2.)

Maps. It is possible to climb only on small local outcrops and never have to refer to a map, but normally some map reading will be required, particularly on the higher hills and mountains. While climbing on mountain crags, for example, a route may finish fairly high on the hill. The weather can change, bringing in visibility-sapping clouds or mist. Some navigation may be necessary to descend to the valley. In Britain, most expe-

Mantelshelf

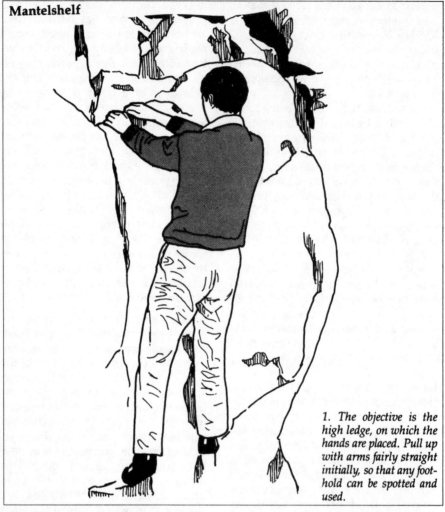

1. *The objective is the high ledge, on which the hands are placed. Pull up with arms fairly straight initially, so that any foothold can be spotted and used.*

ditions will be adequately carried out using the 1:50,000 scale Ordnance Survey (OS) maps. These can be purchased at any large bookshop or specialist outdoor shop, and a good guidebook will give the maps covering the area described in the guide. There are larger scale maps available for the popular areas.

Climbing outside one's home country is never as simple. Again, however, a good specialist shop should stock foreign maps, and can order others. Some countries are guarded regarding maps, which may, in any case, be ancient or poorly surveyed. Expedition reports often help here, and the value of certain publications, such as the *Alpine Journal*, the *Himalayan Journal* and so on will be realized, in pointing one to the right source. Club libraries will also be a good source of information. **Tip.** Buy or borrow the journals of the big climbing clubs — the address of their librarian will be there and access may be gained to a library nearby which could save much time. Having found your map, it would seem sensible to protect it by some sort of weatherseal.

Mantelshelf

2. Raising the body and pressing down on ledge so that the body weight is brought over the hands. The feet help all they can, even if only by smearing on a friction hold.

At its simplest this could be a poly bag. An outdoor shop might sell a map sealant, usually a silicone spray. See also *bearing* and *compass*.

Meditation. With many climbers, some unconscious meditation is done before launching out on a climb. Often the very act of preparation, tying onto the harness, gearing up, has become a pre-climb ritual which stills the mind and makes a better physical effort possible. For most climbers it stops there. For some of the top rock athletes, however, it is possible to gain a slight edge over a rock problem by some form of visualization, where a sequence of moves, probably attempted before or known, is climbed in the mind before actually trying it for real. It helps in other sports, it can work in climbing. See *zen*.

Micros. See *chockstones*.

Mixed route. In Scottish usage a winter route which includes a variety of climbing, with both snow and ice climbing and winter buttress tech-

Mantelshelf

3. Until a high step up can be made and the feet brought up on to the ledge.

niques necessary. The Alpine term would permit rock climbing as well as snow and ice climbing. Mixed routes provide great variety and enjoyment, though not to everyone's taste. *Route finding* may be more demanding on a mixed route, which is all part of the fun.

Mountain rescue. Many countries have an organized system for mountain rescue. In Britain there are rescue teams set up by the police and by the RAF, as well as civilian teams in the popular mountain areas. A complex rescue will often involve co-operation between all three. The civilian teams are formed by volunteers, usually climbers, and rely on donations to fund equipment needs etc. As most rescues will require the involvement of a mountain rescue

team, the prime requirements for climbers on the spot are *first aid* for the injured, the security of the injured, and the accurate and speedy reporting of the accident through the police. See *insurance*.

Moving together. To climb a pitch, or section of a route, moving simultaneously while still joined by the rope. Also called moving in Alpine fashion. For convenience the ropes are shortened by coiling so that the leader or both climbers have coils slung over shoulders. There will be about 3–6m between climbers. See *crevasse rescue* for method of tying on. The second's main task is to maintain a free-running rope and be constantly ready to quickly arrange a temporary belay, eg, by flicking the rope behind a flake. Many climbers will solo easier ground, though moving together can provide a good level of protection when done correctly.

Munro. The original compiler of the list of Scottish mountains over 3000 ft which are now called the Munros. Sir Hugh T. Munro, Bt. (1856-1919) was an original member of the Scottish Mountaineering Club (SMC). There are over 270 Munros, and over 500 tops. Ironically, Munro himself was two short of completing them. The climbing of the Munros is very popular with hill walkers and mountaineers, with a list of 'completers' published annually in the *Scottish Mountaineering Club Journal*. To date, over 600 have admitted 'completion'.

Nails. Boots with soles studded with metal nails, designed to provide a better purchase on the ground and also to be used with small rock holds. Until about the late 1950s, many mountaineers climbed in summer and winter with nailed boots. There were many types of nails, perhaps the best known being the tricouni, after its three-headed design. Nailed boots could be quite effective in winter, particularly on *mixed routes*, though they were soon superseded by *Vibrams* which were lighter and warmer.

Naismith's Rule. A useful guide for hill walkers, giving an indication of the time required for a walk. Originated by Willie Naismith, a founder member of the SMC, it was first published in 1892, and states that the time allowed for an easy expedition should be an hour for every three miles (4.83km) on the map, with an additional hour for every 2,000 ft (607m) of ascent.

Névé. French term for snow ice. This is firm, hard snow which has under-

gone several cycles of thawing and re-freezing. It is one of the very best materials for winter climbing, and is more reliably found on the higher hills in Britain. Mountains which are too high for thawing to occur, or have too high a snowfall, will be unlikely to develop snow as good as this, though on slopes where the sun is plentiful hard snow, leading to ice, may develop. See *water ice.*

New route. See *first ascent.*

Nut key. A useful rock climbing tool developed in the 1980s for dislodging *chockstones* and *friends* too well jammed. It is shaped like a thin spanner, with later models such as that by DMM having two hooks on the end specifically designed for removing friends, which have a habit of becoming jammed. Though a nuisance to

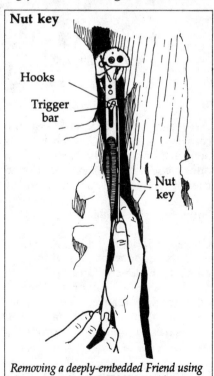

Nut key

Hooks

Trigger bar

Nut key

Removing a deeply-embedded Friend using the two hooks on a DMM nut key.

Off-width

Here, the climber is attempting an awkward, off-width crack using an arm bar, with the left shoulder pressed against the left wall and arm braced against the right wall. The right foot is helping, jammed across the crack, heel on one wall, toe against the other.

carry, best being attached by a thin cord to the harness, it can save its own cost very quickly, particularly if one comes across an abandoned friend!

Nuts. See *chockstones*.

Objective dangers. These are hazards which are apparent on a climb, eg, rock fall, avalanche, and over which the climber has little or no control, other than avoidance. They are common in the Alps, where certain routes have a reputation for rock fall etc.

Off-width. A parallel-sided crack which is too wide to permit *jamming*, yet too narrow to allow *bridging* or back and foot. This particular horror is common in the granite areas of the United States, though uncommon in British climbing. One useful technique for climbing an off-width crack is the arm-bar. Push one arm and shoulder into the crack, and with the arm approximately horizontal bend the elbow and push the palm of the hand into the wall; the shoulder presses against the other wall. Other permutations of arm geometry and opposing pressures will be seen on experimenting. See *jamming*.

Oiled cotton. Wax-impregnated, waterproof cotton material which makes an excellent *anorak*. It is breathable yet waterproof, just as *Gore-tex*. Its only disadvantages are that it is heavier than nylon, and that wearing it might associate one with the green welly brigade.

On sight. To lead a route having no prior, intimate knowledge of its details. The cleanest way to make a *first ascent*, but one now usually re-served for the easier climbs, as tech-nical demands from the hardest climbs approach the limits of human possibility.

Outcrops. Short and usually low level rock crags suitable for climbing through much of the year. In Britain there is a long tradition of outcrop climbing, particularly on the tough gritstone crags of north and central England, while other countries have similarly famous outcrops. Depend-ing on the height of the outcrop and local practice, the routes may be *top roped* or soloed.

Overhand knot. A simple knot of medium strength (67% in a sling) which is sometimes tied instead of a *figure-of-eight*. It is best avoided, how-ever, as following loading it can be very difficult to untie.

Overhang. Rock or ice mass which leans out past the vertical. Over-hangs come in all shapes and sizes but most create a problem. In winter they are often formed at the top of a gully or snow slope as a *cornice*, while a snow or ice overhang may form in a steep gully. Rock overhangs, if short, may be overcome by a *mantel-shelf* move. Keep the feet high under the overhang and on holds or using friction for as long as possible. This helps to conserve strength, which will be draining away all the while. Runners should be spotted and if possible fixed while still under the

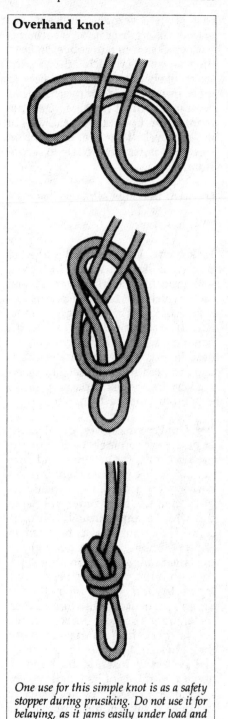

Overhand knot

One use for this simple knot is as a safety stopper during prusiking. Do not use it for belaying, as it jams easily under load and will then be difficult to untie.

roof of the overhang. Prevent *rope drag* by using *extenders*. Overhangs with cracks often jam ropes, so keep them away from each other if that looks likely. Once the decision to move over the bulge or overhang has been made, don't hesitate. Keep the momentum up and shift the weight up and over. If the feet come off at this point it may be too late to reconsider.

Oxygen. See *high altitude climbing*.

PAs. See *boots*.

Pack frame. Metal frame designed to be carried like a rucksack. Indeed, it will normally be sold with an integral sack, which can be removed for carrying bulky or awkward loads. Favoured particularly by North Americans, its extra weight and inflexible shape is a major disadvantage, though it has a place in carrying very heavy loads, perhaps on an expedition approach march.

Peg. Until the mid-1970s, metal pitons or pegs were routinely carried on the harder climbs for belaying and runners. With the improvement in alternative protection devices including nuts, their use in summer, at least in the UK, became virtually obsolescent. They continue to be used in winter climbing and in climbing in the larger ranges including the Alps. As with nuts, pegs have been developed beyond their original basic design, particularly with advances in metallurgy. The best cracks for peg belays are normally horizontal, with the right size of peg being one which can be easily inserted by hand to about two-thirds of its length before a *peg hammer* becomes necessary to hammer it fully home. The various modern designs of pegs include blades, which are for thin cracks; lost

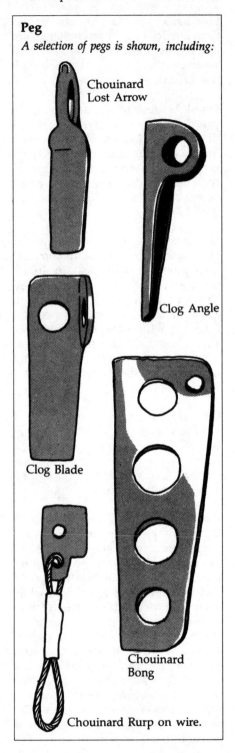

Peg

A selection of pegs is shown, including:

Chouinard Lost Arrow

Clog Angle

Clog Blade

Chouinard Bong

Chouinard Rurp on wire.

arrows, which are thicker; angles, which have a V-shaped cross-section, and bongs, which take the place of wooden *wedges*, and are large V-shaped pegs. The Rurp, an American designed thin, flat peg, is now sold with an attached steel cable. It is intended for incipient cracks, and for aid climbing where it may take the weight of a climber but no more.

Peg hammer. See *hammer*.

Peel. Climbing slang for a fall, probably deriving from 'to peel a fruit'.

Penberthy knot. This is a friction knot used for the same purposes as a *Prusik* knot. It has the advantage over the Prusik knot in being less likely to jam, but as it has to be tied with a length of accessory cord, the ends of which are then tied together to complete a loop, it takes much longer, and is less often used.

Pendulum. A technique in which an otherwise inaccessible part of a face is gained by swinging across using the rope running through a higher belay. Rarely needed except on some of the big wall climbs in North America, especially in Yosemite, where parallel crack systems separated by blank walls may be gained by pendulum. For a big pendulum, the climber may have to increase the amplitude of swing by running from side to side. On a small scale, such as may be needed in the Alps, a pendulum may only require a move or two. It may be required in descent as well as ascent, for example in order to gain a belay ledge for the next abseil (but be aware of the rope running across a sharp edge). If required during an abseil, the climber should be protected by friction knots, as both hands may be needed on the rock.

Pillar. A steep rock feature, usually a slim column standing apart from the main mass of rock and perhaps attached to it by a narrow neck or *arête*.

Pinch grip. A rock hold in which the fingers and sometimes the palms rely heavily on friction for a placement, squeezing the rock like the spine of a book. The hold will therefore vary from good to awful. Standard holds fade into pinches; if you can hook your fingers round a hold it isn't a pinch, if you have to oppose fingers of fingers and thumb then it probably is. Pinch holds often help on *arêtes*, particularly where the rounded edge has to be used. A *layaway* movement used in conjunction with pinches is often successful in such a situation.

Pinch grip

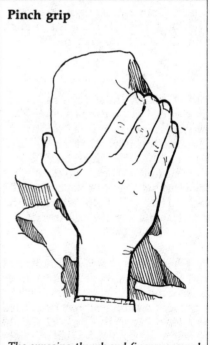

The opposing thumb and fingers grasped round a pinch grip hold. This example shows a fairly wide hold.

Pocket hold

Small cavities, or pockets, in a wall may provide good holds. Here the first three fingers can be used.

Pitch. Section of a route led between belays. Can vary in length up to 50m. The hardest pitch on a multi-pitch route is called the *crux* pitch.

Piton. See *peg*.

Pocket hold. Small cavities in the rock form pocket holds, allowing varying amounts of finger insertion. The smallest may allow part of one finger only to be inserted. The remaining fingers should be closed and the wrist held, if possible, against the rock. This will help alleviate the forces acting on the tendons of the wrist and finger.

Polythene (Poly) bags. Different sizes and strengths of these are invaluable aids for the well-dressed climber. The biggest and strongest may be carried as a *bivvy bag* in the sack. It should be able to accommodate two in a tight squeeze. Next down in size can be used as a sack liner, protecting the contents from damp. A fertilizer bag, preferably unused or at least well-cleaned, is strong enough and about the right size for this purpose. It will last for years if crampons etc are not poked through it. Smaller poly bags have thousands of uses, from protecting maps, spare batteries, food etc, to carrying litter home from the hill or crag.

Porter. Person, usually a native, paid to carry a load towards or on a mountain, commonly in the Himalaya and other higher ranges. Large Himalayan *expeditions* especially provide much useful income for the local hill people, with the high altitude, skilled carrying often being dominated by the Sherpa group. Most porters are paid off on gaining *base camp*, after which the climbers on the expedition will do most of the carrying between camps.

Powder snow. Unconsolidated snow commonly found in cold conditions blowing loose or falling down a slope. Small crystal fragments of ice which cause much discomfort when they effortlessly find any exposed skin or gap in clothing. In a gully there may be a continuous flow of powder, known as *spindrift*, which can make an ascent impossible.

Protection. The placement of *chockstones* and other techniques for good protection is, or should be, one of the pleasures and delights taken by a good leader. Many factors must be taken into consideration. The runners must be placed so as to allow the ropes free movement. The strength of the runner will normally be dictated by the size of the chockstone and the strength of the sling on which the nut is mounted, but the rock may limit the size of nut. With the smallest sizes of chockstones, the rock itself may become a limiting fac-

Protection

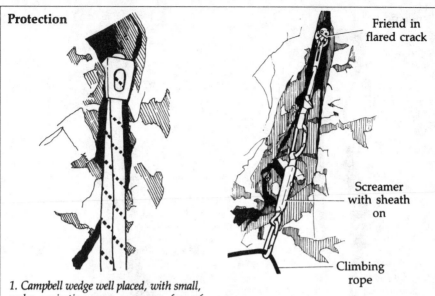

Friend in flared crack

Screamer with sheath on

Climbing rope

1. *Campbell wedge well placed, with small, rocky projection over scoop on face of chockstone.*

2. *A Friend 2½ in a flared crack, in conjunction with a DMM Screamer extender.*

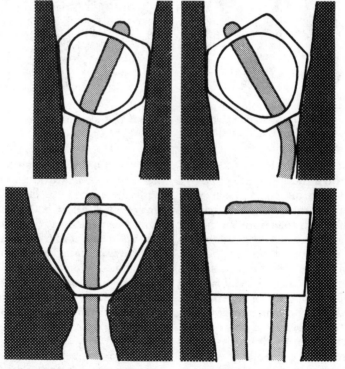

3. *The four possible configurations obtainable using a Hexentric chockstone. See text for explanation.*

Protection

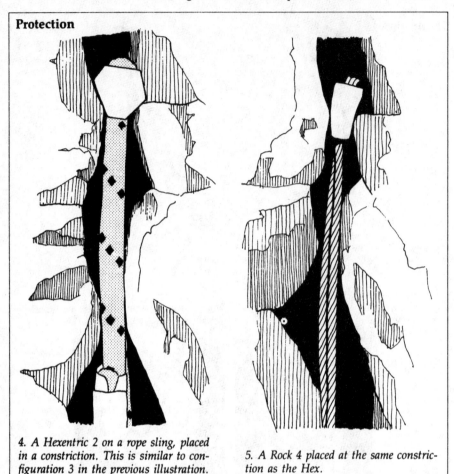

4. *A Hexentric 2 on a rope sling, placed in a constriction. This is similar to configuration 3 in the previous illustration.*

5. *A Rock 4 placed at the same constriction as the Hex.*

tor, with small projections being easily broken on a sudden loading. Full-strength slings on good flakes or used as thread runners will provide some of the best protection. Runners should be placed at fairly regular intervals, the most important point being to place the first one fairly soon after leaving the belay. See *fall factor.* Look at the geometry of the ropes and consider whether an *extender* will be needed to avoid rope *drag.*

The route taken by the ropes will be dictated by the geometry of the pitch and the placement of runners. If a pitch includes a *traverse* then it makes good sense to place a runner at the start of the traverse, to protect the second. Additional runners might be placed further along the traverse, to protect both leader and second as necessary. See *double rope technique.* On a hard traverse a second might wish for a *back rope* to be arranged.

Placing a chockstone in a crack demands some thought. It may take some while before experience allows you to size up a crack and select the right nut. Very often, even for experienced climbers, the first guess will be wrong. It's part of the fun. Try to find the largest nut which fits any particular crack, and try to find a spot in the crack just above and behind a narrowing. The *wedge* will allow itself to be jammed in two ways, placing either the wide or narrow faces against the rock. Always use the wide faces in preference, unless forced to jam it with its narrower end faces in contact with the rock. Used with the narrower ends it can swivel more readily. Place the nut above the selected spot and pull it down until it seats comfortably. If it moves around easily with a gentle pull then it may require re-siting or a stronger pull to seat properly. Try to avoid pushing a nut in deep, it may not come out again and will certainly give your poor second considerable trouble. When placing a nut in a complex crack, remember the sequence of movements so that your second can reverse them on removal.

The curved wedges, eg, Rocks, are superior to the older flat-faced design, as they exert a gentle camming action when placed in a crack. Those with scooped faces should be fitted round small bumps in the crack if possible, which will secure the nut even more firmly, preventing it from being easily pulled out. Always think ahead — from which direction would a pull come from if I fell? In a horizontal crack is the sling protected from any sharp edges? Would two opposed chockstones be better than one at this point? There might be something to be said for the 'cluster theory', the placing of a group of two or three runners close together, particularly when all of the placements are poor or the smallest runners are all that can be found: as long as a pull on one runner will not remove a second.

Many textbooks advocate stacking chockstones together. This smacks of showmanship rather than practicality, as stacked chockstones are easily dislodged. And if you can stack two chockstones together, wide face to wide face, then you can usually insert one bigger nut, end faces to the rock.

Wire chockstones are placed in the same fashion, except that their wire allows them to be placed deeper and

Protection

6. *A Stopper 6 in the same position again. All three of these nuts give an adequate placement; perhaps the hex would be the most secure as it is on a rope sling and would not be moved as easily as the two wire nuts. On the other hand, the strength of the wire nuts would be greater. Place the wire nuts carefully, using extenders, as one good strategy, replace the accessory cord on the hex with kevlar as another.*

Protection

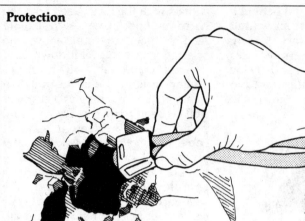

7. *Protection and cunning. Here a Cassin Half-Moon 4, similar to a Rock, is about to be placed in a rock pocket. The chockstone is inserted in the horizontal plane as indicated...*

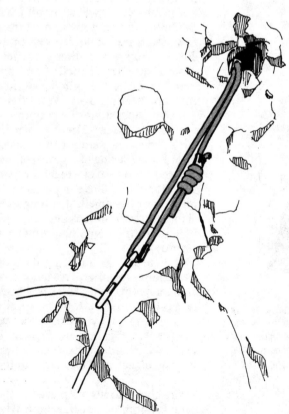

8. *...then given a 90 degrees rotation to jam securely in the pocket. A good, 'bombproof' placement, as long as the sling does not run over a sharp edge.*

Protection

9. When using a micro-wire, in this case a small stopper, the best placement in a crack will be found at a constriction.

10. A large chockstone used in its biggest configuration. A Hexentric 9 used lengthwise. A constriction in the crack is necessary, as there is no camming action when used in this way.

11. A well-placed Friend 1½. The Friend is positioned so as to be aligned with the probable direction of pull in a fall. The sling ensures that the rope is well clear of the crack, and that movement of the rope will affect the sling but not the Friend.

Protection

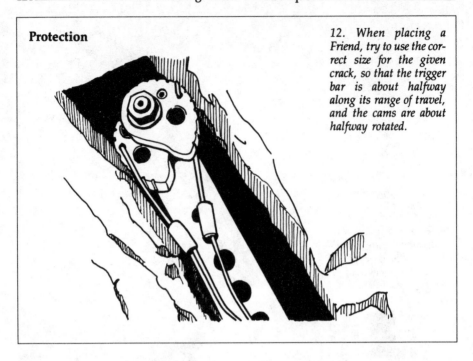

12. When placing a Friend, try to use the correct size for the given crack, so that the trigger bar is about halfway along its range of travel, and the cams are about halfway rotated.

higher. As they can be placed where no fingers can reach, they can be very difficult to remove using the wire alone. A *nut key* can help remove such awkward customers, but try to avoid inserting them too deeply in the first case. One major disadvantage of wire chockstones is the swivelling action imparted by the climbing rope. This can dislodge a wire nut, making it even more important to use an *extender*. Small wired chockstones, *micros*, are easily dislodged, and in any case will not be able to withstand much of a pull. In many cases the wire and nut hold together, but the actual rock fails, its small projections snapping off. The small micros should be placed so that the maximum area is in contact with the rock, to spread the load and help prevent the head shearing under load. When removing micros, be aware that the weak point is where the cables enter the head. Do not tug the wire up and down to remove it,

especially when it is well jammed, as this can split the cables at that point. Use a *nut key* instead, and work on the head.

Hexentrics are better in the middle to large sizes, making them particularly useful on easier routes and on routes with wider cracks. Due to their clever asymmetric design they have, like curved *wedges*, a camming effect in a crack, and a choice of no less than four positions from which to choose. Position one provides a slight taper with a little camming action, position two a greater taper and camming action (effectively half a size greater), position three is for a constriction in a crack, while fourth position is the chockstone used at its widest setting, when it becomes a simple wedge.

Hexentrics (hexes) were designed with the smooth granite cracks of Yosemite in mind, and in a sense they are a forerunner of the mechanically camming *friends*. The first hexentrics were designed by Chouinard in 1971. Two years later the polycentric hexentric emerged, the asymmetric design used today. Hexes come in sizes 1 through 11, with the top sizes being fairly unwieldy. If one particular size is too small for a crack and the next size too large, then rotate the smaller size into its wider position, when it will effectively become half a size larger.

If you see a hard section of climbing coming up ahead then consider putting in a runner before reaching the spot. You will be reasonably protected, and will not be under as much psychological pressure. By all means use what you find at the hard spot, if you can hang about without too much difficulty. Many runners will have to be arranged with one hand, as the other hand will be engaged in hanging on!

Prusik knot. Friction knot invented by an Austrian climber, Dr Prusik. It is perhaps one of the most useful knots to learn, being particularly important for self-rescue and ascending a fixed rope. See *crevasse rescue*. It is tied using a loop of accessory cord, with 6mm diameter cord suitable for both 9 and 11mm climbing ropes. Its main rivals are the 'user-friendly' *Bachmann* or *Klemheist* knots, which are conveniently used in conjunction with a karabiner. Disadvantages are its tendency to jam under a loading, and a disconcerting possibility of failing under a shock loading.

Psychological runner. The placement of protection which is known to be poor, but whose existence gives a leader a psychological 'boost', often enough to make the difference between failure or success. This mild example of self-delusion is acceptable in moderation. Leaders who insist on continuing to lead on a succession of

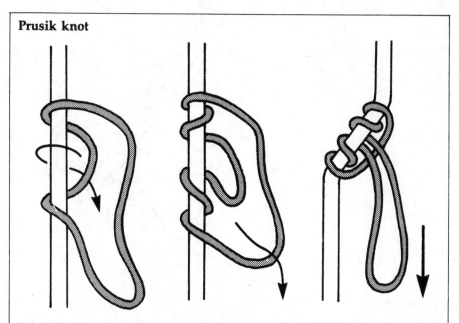

Prusik knot

A useful friction knot, for self-rescue when climbing a rope is necessary. When tying the knot, keep the strands symmetrical on the climbing rope.

such runners soon find it difficult to obtain seconds.

Pulley system. There are two occasions when some sort of a hoist arrangement might be needed to help a belayed climber lift a heavy load:

a) when a fallen climber has to be hoisted up a face, or out of a *crevasse*,

b) when a heavy sack has to be hauled up a pitch.

In both cases a combination of *prusik* loops, *belays* and *karabiners* can give a slight mechanical advantage to the hauler. The simplest technique to help lift a climber uses two karabiners and one prusik loop. The belayer

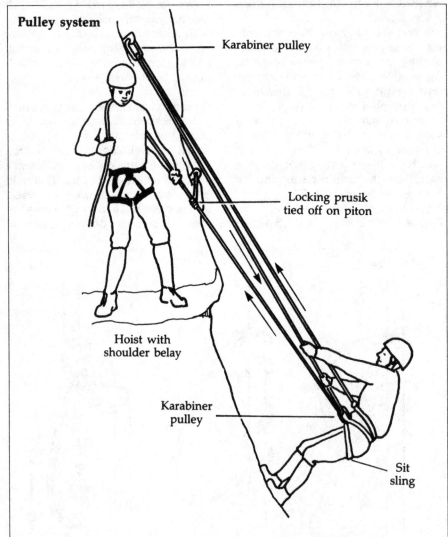

Pulley system

Karabiner pulley

Locking prusik
tied off on piton

Hoist with
shoulder belay

Karabiner
pulley

Sit
sling

1. *The Two Karabiner Pulley. This may be a useful technique for extricating a victim from a crevasse; when, for example, the victim is able to assist and it is possible to use the walls of the crevasse for footholds. See text for explanation.*

Pulley system

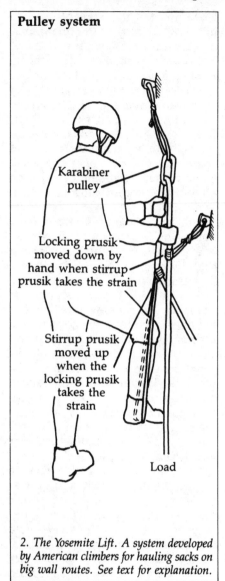

Karabiner pulley

Locking prusik moved down by hand when stirrup prusik takes the strain

Stirrup prusik moved up when the locking prusik takes the strain

Load

2. The Yosemite Lift. A system developed by American climbers for hauling sacks on big wall routes. See text for explanation.

clips in the rope to a belay karabiner then lowers a loop to the bottom climber who will clip the loop into a karabiner conveniently attached to the harness. The rope should now describe an 'S-shape', running from the belayer, through the bottom climber's karabiner, up to the pulley karabiner, then back to the bottom climber's harness. The prusik loop goes on to the rope leading down to the lower climber, and is a fail-safe device. The prusik loop should be attached to a separate belay.

The belayer now begins to hoist by using a shoulder belay, stooping down then taking in rope on straightening up. It is important to avoid personal injury by maintaining a straight back and bending the legs. As the rope is taken in, the prusik loop should be pushed down. The lower climber can assist not only by using footholds to walk up, but by actively pulling on the rope running up from the karabiner to the top karabiner.

For lifting a heavy sack up a face the Yosemite Lift may be used. This requires two prusik loops and one karabiner pulley, with the belayed climber hoisting the load using body weight and a foot-pumping action. One prusik is the locking prusik, attached to the loaded side of the rope and to a belay. The other prusik is for a foot loop. In use, the climber pulls the rope through the karabiner by stepping down on the foot prusik and pulling both ropes with the hands. At the end of a foot pump, the locking prusik loop should be pushed down while the climber's weight takes the load. On lifting the foot, the locking prusik will take the strain and the foot prusik can then be pushed up the rope, ready for the next lifting cycle. **Tip**. Use a *Bachmann* or *Klemheist* knot instead of a prusik, and cushion the foot loop for comfort. There are available small, lightweight pulleys, such as the Petzl range. They can make life much easier if any amount of hauling is planned.

Quarries. Abandoned commercial quarries may provide steep and technical rock climbs. The quality of climbing depends on the rock type and the length of time for which the quarry has been abandoned, as loose rock is often a hazard in a fairly new quarry. Recently developed old slate quarries in Wales are providing very bold climbs up relatively holdless walls, with *bolt* runners becoming a fairly common feature.

Quartz holds. These are found on metamorphic rocks such as gneiss and schist. They should be used with care, as the mineral is brittle and can fracture when pulling up, particularly with a small hold.

Quick draw. See *extenders*.

Rack. Personal collection of protection gear, conveniently grouped together and preferably organized into some system, eg, by size of *chockstone*. For a few years the use of a *bandolier* was popular with rock climbers, a specially made nylon loop carried over one shoulder with a broad section for comfort and a narrow section for clipping *karabiners*. The sole advantage of a bandolier is that most of the gear can be quickly transferred from climber to climber, eg, when exchanging the *lead* on a climb. Disadvantages include the corollary that dropping the bandolier is disastrous, and also that on easy-angled rock it can be a nuisance, tending to swing round to the front and obscure footholds.

Better *harness* design now includes good gear loops, so that most gear is carried that way. Exceptions are long slings, which are carried round the neck or over one shoulder. Carrying slings over one shoulder stops them swinging in front, though they can then only be removed with one hand. Carry a long sling by forming it into a figure-of-eight loop then clipping a karabiner through both loops.

Gear on the harness is best placed in some order. This will make it easier to find the right size of nut in a hurry, which may be important, particularly on a hard, strenuous route. The order is personal, with climbers arriving at a set up which suits their own preference, but as an example of racking the larger nuts and *friends* can go on the left, smaller to the front. Small nuts and wires will then go on the right, along with *extenders* and spare karabiners. Gear not used when actually climbing can also go on the right, towards the back, such as *descenders, nut keys* etc. Extenders should be complete with karabiners. Some climbers carry several *wires* on one karabiner, which makes it slightly faster to select the right size for a crack but adds potential for disaster should the karabiner be dropped. The selected wire then has to be removed from the collection, a krab brought out for use with it and so on. Again, this is a matter of personal preference. The common mistake a novice (and even experienced climbers) makes is to carry insufficient karabiners. It's much more fun to buy a new nut, but false economy often rules out buying the karabiner which should accompany it.

As to the contents of a rack, a beginner will gradually add gear as pocket money allows, though a basic core should include two long, stitched slings with screw gate karabiners for belays, two normal length, stitched slings with ordinary karabiners for runners, one medium and one large *hexentric*, a range of curved wedges, eg, 'Rocks', say four or five, of which the three largest would be attached to accessory cord (usually 8mm) and the remaining two would be bought already wired. Each nut must have its own karabiner, with 2200kg strength being the choice.

With increasing experience, ability, and pocket money, the rack can expand to include several more nuts filling gaps in the ranges already carried, along with a medium-sized friend, perhaps a size 2½ or 3, and several extenders. The final gaps in one's rack will probably be filled with several sizes of friends and a selection of *micros*. These last can be used with 2000kg karabiners. Gear is of course often shared, which can help during the early days, but many climbers like to be autonomous climbing machines, perhaps only borrowing one or two items from their partners and handing them over at each stance. On a day involving a long walk to the cliff it makes sense to rationalize gear to some extent, as long as communication does not break down and both climbers leave behind a crucial item! If a friend is carried it is sensible to carry a *nut key* which has hooks for removing a burrowing *Friend*.

In winter, the make up of a rack is different, with (normally) the smallest nuts being left out. In general fewer nuts will be carried, with only a very few pure snow and ice routes requiring none at all. Those carried will be mainly in the larger sizes. The larger friends remain useful. The same slings should be adequate, with the longer ones being most useful for boulder belays etc. Depending on the route, a *deadman* may be carried, as might be *drive ins* and *ice screws*. Extenders should be used with screws.

Rake. A Lake District term for a long, slanting ledge running across a mountain face.

Rappel. North American term for *abseil*.

Red Point. To practise a route before attempting to lead it. This technique will be found only on the hardest routes, with climbers *top roping* the climb before removing all gear and trying a 'clean' ascent.

Reef knot. Knot used to finish off coiling a rope for scrambling. Can work loose, hence not used for any other purpose in climbing except tying bootlaces.

Rescue. See *mountain rescue*.

Reversing. To climb down a pitch or route. Also known as down climbing. It happens to all climbers. Difficulties are too great, the body tires, the rock is wet. Sometimes a short descent to a resting place is sufficient to recharge tired muscles. On other occasions the route has been abandoned and the decision made to reverse it back down to the start. Finally, many routes are useful in descent, perhaps after another climb has been finished on the same cliff. If the rock is easy, and easy-angled, it is best to descend facing out. The route is more easily seen that way and a slip can be halted by taking the weight on the hands. With increasing steepness and difficulty, the descent is made facing in, as in ascent. The main problem is usually finding footholds, easily spotted on the way up but often partially hidden in descent. Finding good handholds and leaning out on them to find both the holds and the way down can help.

If there are runners on the pitch which has to be reversed then they will provide *protection* on the way down too. If the route can be reversed without too much difficulty then they can be removed as they are reached. The second should take in the ropes carefully so that they do not obstruct the retreat, but not so enthusiastically that they pull on the leader. If the pitch is difficult or the climber

Reversing

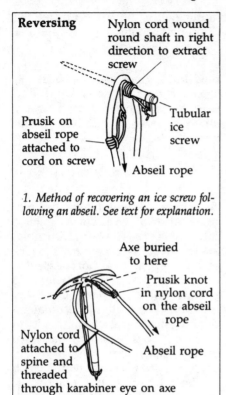

Nylon cord wound round shaft in right direction to extract screw

Tubular ice screw

Prusik on abseil rope attached to cord on screw

Abseil rope

1. *Method of recovering an ice screw following an abseil. See text for explanation.*

Axe buried to here

Prusik knot in nylon cord on the abseil rope

Nylon cord attached to spine and threaded through karabiner eye on axe

Abseil rope

2. *Method of recovering an ice axe used to belay an abseil. See text for explanation.*

unhappy then at least one good runner will have to be left in for protection, preferably at the highest point. If necessary the leader can be lowered down to the *belay* from this runner. A leader who has run out too much rope before deciding to retreat will not reach the belay, on a lower. The decision will be between climbing down to an intermediate belay, or abseiling from a secure high point, having pulled up the ropes from a securely belayed second.

If the climb is being abandoned other runners can be removed during the lower. There will be so much friction with a *belay plate* and runner that there should be no difficulty lowering a leader safely. On reaching

the belay clip in before recovering the rope. It is of course possible to reverse a route roped together and putting in runners. In this case, the stronger climber should be last, ie, the higher of the two.

Down climbing is a necessary part of a climber's repertoire. It would be very difficult and certainly impossibly slow to do any of the classic ridge walks and scrambles without some down climbing being involved.

Reversing in winter has its own problems, protection often being harder to arrange. On easier routes footholds should be obvious, which is half the battle. If it is necessary to be lowered from a runner, be aware that ice screws under a load will slowly melt away the supporting ice. Always try to find a secure rock belay. There are two cunning methods of retrieving winter anchors following an abseil (though it is difficult to find anyone who has actually used them). The first allows an *ice screw* to be recovered following an abseil. Insert the screw most, but not all of the way, leaving it with the eye uppermost. Now attach accessory cord to the eye then wind the cord round the shaft of the screw, finally attaching the end to a *prusik* loop on one of the ropes, using the side which when pulled from below will have the effect of unwinding the cord and unscrewing the ice screw. There should be sufficient length of cord to allow the screw to be fully unscrewed.

The second method is to allow the retrieval of a vertically placed *ice axe*. Attach a cord to the spike of the axe (most modern axes have an eye just above the spike). The cord then runs up the shaft and through the hole which should be near the head, if not actually running through it. It then attaches to a prusik loop on one of the ropes. Remember which rope, so that when pulled on there should be an upward force on the axe, allowing it to be pulled out. Be careful to avoid being brained by the falling axe.

Rhyolite. A rough, volcanic rock providing excellent rock climbing. Much of Glencoe and Lake District climbing is on this rock.

Rib. A projecting spine of rock, of varying sizes, but normally steeper than an *arête*.

Ridge. A large rock feature on a mountain, normally the crest formed where two faces meet. Easy angled ridges provide exhilarating scrambling and walking, while the steeper ridges often provide good climbs.

River crossing. This may be necessary in rough country where bridges may be absent or far between. In Scotland particularly, many long walks include the necessity to ford a river or burn. During dry weather all but the larger rivers will provide little difficulty; it is in wet weather with swollen and fast-flowing streams that trouble can happen. For slow and shallow crossings with no stepping stones, many walkers will remove boots and socks. A confident walker will even throw boots over a narrow stream before crossing, though this is obviously tempting fate. (The rationale is that if they are knotted and hung round one's neck, they could be dropped if you stumble). As the stream becomes larger, faster and rougher underfoot, it will probably pay to remove socks but replace the boots, which will allow the feet to obtain a more secure purchase underwater. If there are dry boulders and you are nimble enough, then boulder hopping a stream is a viable way of crossing. Plan the route before setting out, as it is often a dynamic experience, with continuous move-

ment often necessary. Be aware of the penalty for a slip however.

Do not attempt to ford the faster streams or go over thigh depth unless it is possible to rope up, and then only if a search for a safer crossing has proved fruitless. Too many have drowned thinking they could make it. Belay before crossing and make a diagonal crossing going down with the current. Face partly upstream. Look for shallower areas, where the crossing may be longer but safer. Undo the rucksack waist band; if you go under you may wish to abandon it rather than stay under. A long stick or pole can help balance, otherwise move across with a shuffling gait, trying to keep the feet low while they search for a secure foothold. Once over, move upstream a little to compensate for the diagonal movement and belay the next person. **Tip**. If you can hear rocks and boulders moving then the stream is almost certainly too dangerous for a crossing — keep walking until a safer spot is found. A half-day detour may be inconvenient, but much less so than death or serious injury.

Rock boots. See *boots*.

Rock climbing. One area of climbing specializing in the ascent of rock routes. The other main area is snow and ice climbing. Occasionally a route, particularly in the Alps, may combine both, though it is normal to have them separate. Many, if not most climbers, engage in rock climbing only, given the ready availability of rock.

Rock types. The various types of rock climbed on are mentioned under their respective letters and include; *andesite, basalt, gabbro, gneiss, granite, limestone, rhyolite, sandstone, schist* and *slate*.

Rognons. Rocky islands in a *glacier*, often providing safe areas for bivouacs or huts.

Roof. The underside of a large *overhang*. Often provides a major obstacle on a climb, perhaps requiring *aid* or a diversion to overcome it. In the Alps a roof may provide shelter for a bivouac, though be aware of possible *lightning* hazard.

Rope. **a)** A party of climbers connected by a rope. **b)** The actual rope used for climbing, usually of *kernmantel* construction. **c)** To rope up, to tie on to the climbing rope preparatory to climbing.

Route. **a)** A defined climb or line, often described in a *guidebook*. **b)** A walk or longer trip by foot.

Route card. The systematic description of a planned walk, often used by organized outdoor groups as a navigational aid and for safety should an incident arise. School and outdoor centre groups use route cards, which break down a walk into its constituent sections, giving the bearing, length and estimated time for each leg of the walk, along with suggested alternatives in case of bad weather etc. A copy of the route card will then be left at the centre or base, along with details of the party.

Route finding. The art of working out where a climb goes. Some routes may require virtually no route finding, perhaps following some very obvious feature such as a crack or chimney. Other routes may be quite devious, having to zig-zag up a complex face or buttress. Normally the bigger the face or mountain, the more route finding will be required. Route finding improves with experience, though some climbers are better than

others. For many it is one of the great pleasures in mountaineering. Route finding requires the ability to 'read' the features of a climb, to deduce where the holds are best, where the protection is and whether belays are available. It faces its most difficult test when attempting a *first ascent*.

On an existing climb, particularly one described in a *guidebook*, much of the work has already been done, though hopefully some route finding is still required by the climber. There will be other clues as to a route's line, such as the almost ubiquitous *chalk* marks on holds, particles of wool, and, regretfully, perhaps litter on belay stances. Popular routes will probably be obvious by polished holds and cleaner rock in general.

Rucksack. Nylon or canvas bag designed for carrying climbing and walking equipment and incorporating shoulder straps for carrying. For heavy loads while walking, eg, on an *expedition* approach, a *pack frame* may be useful, otherwise a sack without a frame is used for climbing. Apart from a basic shape, which is often a 'squared off' cylinder, a good sack will have a padded back and shoulder straps for comfortable carrying, a reinforced base, straps for attaching two axes, and a lid with a zip-fastened pocket for quick access to small necessities. Anything else is usually superfluous, though a built-in extension can be useful in a *bivouac*, allowing the lower part of the body to be protected by the sack. Another useful feature is the ability to have some attachment point for tying on a *camping mat*.

Many climbing sacks have attachment points for *crampons*. For winter climbing in Britain these usually cause more danger than create convenience, though for Alpine climbing they probably allow quick access to the crampons. There is now a bewildering range of sacks, in many sizes from small walker's day sacks, to climbing day sacks, to weekend-sized sacks, to monster-sized sacks. The ideal size is one which allows day walks, day climbs, and weekend camping trips. **Tip**. The larger the rucksack you use, the more equipment you will carry. Do you need all that gear? Could you use a smaller sack?

Runner. See *protection*.

Running. See *training*.

Run-out. The amount of *rope* used by a *leader* on a pitch. A full run-out uses all available rope, when the leader must find a suitable belay. The *second* has the responsibility of informing the leader how much rope is left towards the end of a pitch, so that the leader can begin to look for a belay. A long run-out with no protection is a serious lead, given the consequences of a fall.

Sack-hauling. On very steep and long routes, eg, the big wall routes in Yosemite, a leader will climb without sack, hauling it up the pitch once belayed. For this purpose, most rucksacks are provided with a hauling loop. Specially designed hauling domes are also available, to protect a sack from the ravages of being hauled. For convenience, sack-hauling is best done using some sort of a *pulley system*.

Safety rope. A rope used to protect a climber during a potentially hazardous manoeuvre. Most commonly used during an *abseil*, when the climber will be descending using a double rope and will also be protected by a separate safety rope, paid out by another climber normally tied on to another belay. Often used because the abseil belay is doubtful, the rock hazardous or belays at the bottom of the abseil uncertain. Beginners gaining experience at abseiling are best protected with a safety rope.

Sandstone. A sedimentary rock, formed by grains of quartz held together by a cement. Soft sandstone weathers very readily and can be very loose, but the harder varieties can give excellent climbing, often of a strenuous nature, with steep walls and rounded holds. The magnificent hills in the north-west of Scotland, formed of Torridonian sandstone, have some impressive buttresses formed by this dark red rock.

Schist. A metamorphic rock often formed into beautiful folds. This rock was probably initially deposited in a shallow sea. Deposition of sediments could vary from day to day, with slow, gentle deposition giving fine layers, and a flood or marine slide forming a conglomerate. They were then subjected to great heat and pressure from overlying deposits, deforming and hardening. Layers formed could be maintained through later changes, so that today we see layered rocks, with scalloped holds perhaps formed by the slightly different rates of weathering between the layers. They often have a high *quartz* content, with associated bands of the white mineral.

Scoop. A shallow depression in a rock face, sometimes providing a resting place on an otherwise strenuously steep wall.

Scrambling. Easy rock allows rapid, unroped movement, known as scrambling. Many of the classic British ridges require long stretches of scrambling for speed, where the hands are occasionally required but the technical difficulty does not warrant the use of a rope.

Screamer. See *extenders*.

Scree. Loose, rocky debris lying under cliffs and on hillsides with rocky outcrops which have eroded. Some famous scree slopes, often known as 'shoots', can provide fast, exciting 'runs', though all require some care. Many gullies have scree lying in their beds, which can be a problem for climbers who have to avoid knocking down rocks onto other climbers. The technique used for scree-running is one based on leaning forward to keep the weight over the boots, keeping the legs bent and springy, and digging in the heels which then slide down one at a time.

Screw gate. See *karabiner*.

Sea cliffs. The coast of Britain and many other countries provides a huge extent of steep cliff and sea stack climbing, much of it undeveloped. While many sea cliffs are formed of badly eroding rock, there are worthwhile areas. Unique problems found are difficulty of access, *birds*, and expensive ferry charges. Another problem can be the rapid corrosion of aluminium alloy equipment such as *karabiners*, due to the high salt content of sea air. Wash such equipment after climbing on a sea cliff. If climbing on certain *sea stacks*, it might help to refer to tide tables before setting out. Some stacks can only be reached at low tide. The converse, that access may be cut off by high tide, does not seem to be obvious to everyone. A rope may be left attached to the mainland in some cases, allowing a *Tyrolean traverse* to provide an escape. If a small boat is available then many of the problems may be eased, and some new ones created! It may well be worth hiring a local boat operator who will know local conditions and be grateful for extra income.

Sea stack. Isolated pinnacle of rock rising out of the sea, often being originally part of a mainland sea cliff which has become separated from the parent mass through erosion. Very often a stack will be formed first as an arch, then, on the bridge collapsing, promotion to a stack occurs. See *sea cliffs*.

Second. a) One half of a climbing pair, the other climber being the *leader*. A balanced pair will often share the lead, taking it in turns to lead. The climber not leading a pitch will second it, belaying the leader to begin with. The main task of the second is to manage the ropes and belay safely, letting the leader know how much rope is available and keeping an eye on the smooth running of the ropes. A second will encourage a leader, within safe bounds of course!

b) A second is about how much time is available in order to begin ice axe *braking* during a fall.

Self-protection. Arrangement of security when soloing. This is fairly straightforward when a one *pitch* route on an outcrop has to be protected by a solo cliimber. The most usual way is to fix a rope to a good *belay* on top of the route then climb with a *prusik* or *jumar* type device, sliding it up the rope as you progress. The lower end of the rope is conveniently kept on the ground with a moderate weight, not so much that you cannot shift the rope over if necessary but enough to allow the prusik to slide up without lifting the rope too.

There are several good devices on the market, eg, Jumar, Clog and Petzl makes. All can take 9 or 11mm *ropes*, single or double, though not a 9 and 11mm at the same time. An efficient method using such a device, which normally has both a lower and an upper *karabiner* attachment point, is to connect the harness to the lower point, and a chest sling or harness to the upper point. On climbing up, the chest sling, worn like a *bandolier*, should pull the device up the rope without any need to use hands, while in the event of a fall you should be suspended comfortably in the harness. The Petzl Croll is designed to be used with a waist and chest harness, while the Petzl Shunt may be used with a waist or sit harness only. Needless to say, mistakes will be punished, and no device is totally fail-proof. Prusik knots themselves can fail on a shock loading, which has injured and killed climbers using them for self-protection. A good *ascender* is better but still not invincible.

Self-protection on a multi-pitch route is much more difficult to arrange. The climbing rope must be securely tied on to a belay at the start of each pitch. As runners will be used on pitches this belay must be set up to defend against upward pulls. Tie on to the rope some metres from the belay, the distance along the rope from the belay depending on the nature of the climb and on how big a fall you are prepared to face! A *figure-of-eight* knot on to the harness is required. You are now, in effect, leading on a short rope attached directly to a belay. Fix runners as you lead. Before the rope comes tight, pull in more slack rope and tie on to a second figure-of-eight, exchanging this for the first and repeating as necessary until the next belay is gained. Now *abseil* down the pitch,

removing runners and bottom belay, before *prusiking* back up the rope to begin all over again. Obviously, this game is so filled with potential traps that you would have to be pretty determined, if not desperate, to want to try it. Also, think of the consequences of a fall on steep rock. How will you rescue yourself?

Self-rescue. A fall on steep ground may require a climber to regain a belay without climbing being possible. It is also extremely difficult for a climber to be pulled up (though see *pulley system* for some ideas on this method), so that some method of self-help is often necessary. This is normally based on *prusiking* up the

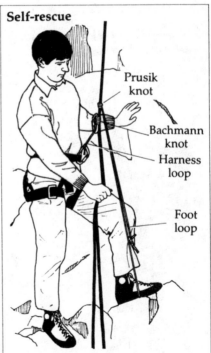

Self-rescue

Prusik knot

Bachmann knot

Harness loop

Foot loop

1. Ascending a doubled rope using two rope loops. In this example, the longer foot cord is attached above the harness cord using a prusik knot. The harness cord is attached using a karabiner and Bachmann knot.

Self-rescue

2. Standing in the foot loop, push the harness cord up the rope.

3. Suspended from the harness cord, push the foot loop up the rope.

rope to regain a stance. In certain circumstances it may be possible, and better, for a fallen climber to be lowered to a suitable stance, the partner then joining up by *abseil*. Falling into a *crevasse* is often followed by self-rescue, with the victim prusiking up the rope using two friction knots pre-tied on to the rope. The *Klemheist knot* is better than a *prusik knot*, though mechanical *ascenders* are better still.

Using any of these devices the method is, however, similar. Two accessory loops will be required, a shorter loop for the harness, and a longer leg loop. The leg loop is attached lower down the rope, with both loops being attached fairly close to the harness. The harness loop is crucial and should be attached using a locking karabiner. With one foot in the leg loop it should be possible to straighten the leg, stand up while suspended from the leg loop prusik, and slide the harness prusik up the rope. Next hang from the harness prusik and slide up the leg loop. Continue this alternation to regain the stance. As friction knots can fail under a shock load, at intervals tie an *overhand knot* in the rope under the lower loop knot. Any failure of the knots leading to a slide down the rope should then be halted by this backup. There should obviously be no runners on the rope. As in *crevasse rescue*, practise self-rescue in a safe and easy environment, eg, a local crag or convenient tree.

Sérac. An isolated pinnacle or tower of ice, commonly found on a *glacier* and especially on *icefalls*. As they are formed by moving ice they are temporary and unstable structures, and should accordingly be treated with great caution.

Sheet bend. Though uncommon, it

Self-rescue

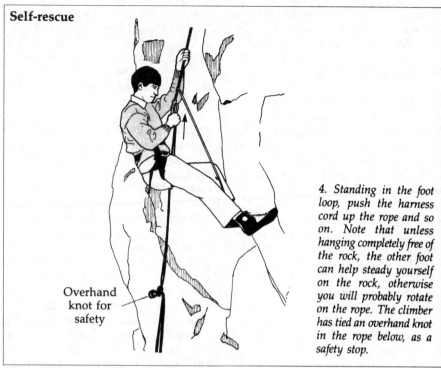

Overhand knot for safety

4. Standing in the foot loop, push the harness cord up the rope and so on. Note that unless hanging completely free of the rock, the other foot can help steady yourself on the rock, otherwise you will probably rotate on the rope. The climber has tied an overhand knot in the rope below, as a safety stop.

might be necessary to join a 9mm rope with an 11mm rope, eg, before making an *abseil*. The sheet bend is also useful for joining two slings of unequal diameters together. The knot is easily adjusted but can also work loose and should be finished off using an *overhand knot*.

Side hold. Rock hold which, though of little use for a down-pull, is good when used laterally. When *laybacking*, for example, most of the handholds used will be side holds. When used on their own or in conjunction with other holds, they are normally working against a foothold, pulling towards the body with the side hold while pushing against a foothold and away from the body. Often used in a dynamic situation.

Siege tactics. To climb a route in sections, leaving fixed ropes during the attempt. Generally condemned as a

Sheet bend

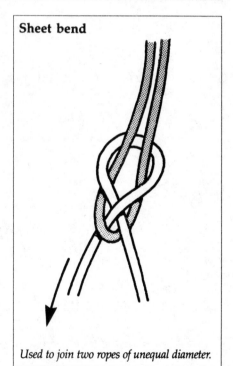

Used to join two ropes of unequal diameter.

tactic, except perhaps in the Himalaya, where big routes would be very difficult without some sieging.

Sit harness. See *harness*.

Sit sling. This is a rudimentary harness quickly made using a standard 25mm nylon *tape* sling. Known in the USA as a swami belt. Though its use is unnecessary now, due to the development of good *sit harnesses*, it might be useful in an emergency where there is no spare harness, eg, rescuing a non-climber. The most comfortable is perhaps the Dulfer. A long tape sling is required. If it is too long then shorten it using an *overhand knot*. Clip a locking *karabiner* into the sling then pass the sling behind the body at waist level. Drop one loop with the karabiner and pull it through between the legs to clip it into the front loops of the sling. If the length is correct there should now be

support for the waist and both thighs. This sit sling, like others, can fall down if unsupported, and if desired it can be combined with a sling tied round the waist, clipping the karabiner into the waist sling as well.

Ski mountaineering. The use of skis to travel over mountainous terrain. This sport neatly bridges winter hill walking and piste skiing, and in the right conditions it allows good distances to be covered over snow-covered mountains. There is a choice of ski type, between the Alpine equipment familiar to piste-bashers, and Nordic, the long, narrow ski used for cross-country skiing. In addition to skis, necessary equipment includes ski-mountaineering boots, skins (allowing movement up steeper hills when fitted over skis), ski crampons, for hard snow or ice, and normal winter hill-walking gear,

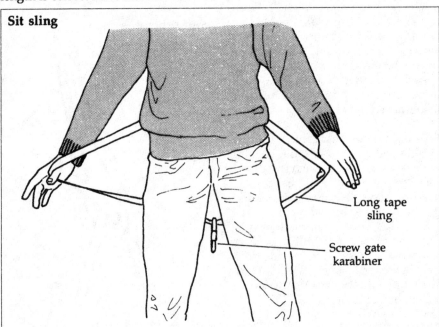

Sit sling

Long tape sling

Screw gate karabiner

1. Forming a sit sling of the Dulfer type. Clip a screw gate karabiner into a long tape sling and pass it behind your body.

Sit sling

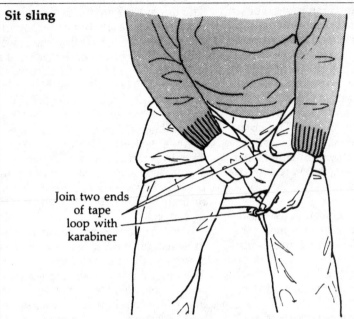

Join two ends
of tape
loop with
karabiner

2. Reach behind and grap the karabiner, then bring together the two ends of the tape loop.

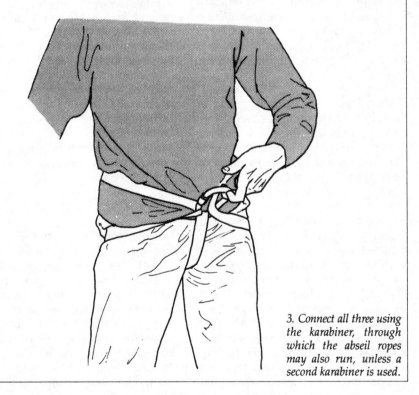

3. Connect all three using the karabiner, through which the abseil ropes may also run, unless a second karabiner is used.

including axe and crampons. The art of good and safe ski mountaineering is probably best based on experience in both skiing and in winter mountaineering. There are difficulties peculiar to ski mountaineering, including accurate navigation while moving faster and more erratically than one would on foot. The ability to ski mountaineer opens up more possibilities for the mountaineer, particularly in the glaciated areas of the world.

Sky hook. Flat metal hook used in *aid climbing*. About 7cm in length, this can be hooked over rock projections and an *étrier* attached. As it is not inserted into a crack, it is only loosely attached and requires care in use.

Slab. An inclined expanse of rock, between about 30 and 75 degrees. It can be any size, from a few metres to hundreds of metres in length. When holds are scarce climbing may have to be done using friction for the feet and anything that can be found for the hands.

Slate. This metamorphic rock is usually climbed on in disused quarries, particularly in Wales, where recent activity has seen climbs of a very high standard. Due to a lack of natural protection, many of the harder climbs need *bolt* runners.

Sleeping bag. Long bag of insulated material, either down or synthetic, encased in a nylon cover and with or without a zip for easy access. Modern designs taper from the shoulders to the feet to conserve material and maximize warmth. The major decision involved in the purchase of a good sleeping bag is whether to buy a synthetic bag or one using duck or goose down. The synthetic bags are heavier but absorb less water if wet.

The down bags are probably still the winner, given a few basic precautions during use. Avoid getting them wet when carrying by keeping them in a poly bag (in addition to their own stuff bag). **Tips**. Use them in conjunction with a cotton sheet liner. You will be more comfortable, and the bag will need to be washed less often and will last much longer. If you do have to wash a down bag then buy a soft detergent made for the purpose. In between use, keep them out of their stuff bag to allow the down to expand.

Bags, like some tents, come defined in 'seasons', with a two-season bag being suitable for the summer only. The ambition is to own a good four-season bag, suitable for winter camping. High expedition use will require a five-season bag, which may be double and will certainly be very well insulated indeed. The insulation of a down bag comes from the air trapped in the minute feathers. Modern synthetic materials try to mimic nature by using long fibres which are hollow. Couples can buy sleeping bags with left and right zips which allows them (the bags!) to be zipped together for mutual warmth.

Sling. Loop of nylon rope or tape, used for belays, runners, abseil loops etc. See *belay*.

Snake sling. See *extenders*.

Snow blindness. Over-exposure to bright sunlight, easily attained on a glacier or Alpine route, can lead to a temporary blindness. This is both painful and potentially awkward. Avoid by wearing good sunglasses or goggles. These should have ultra-violet filters, the choice of colour is yours. **Tip**. Even a cloudy day has UV radiation sparking up your retinal cells; if you are having to squint then you should be wearing protection.

Snow bridge. Frequently found partially covering a *crevasse*, and sometimes allowing a convenient crossing. Never try one without being roped together, belayed, and prepared for the plunge, and take even more care in the afternoon, when all snow structures on a glacier will be at their weakest. Small bridges may be attempted by a brave climber crawling to spread the weight. First climber to cross should then belay on the other side, as no snow bridge can be trusted. See *crevasse rescue*.

Snow hole. A shelter excavated in deep snow, usually as an emergency but sometimes to provide a superior bivouac site on a big mountain. The preparation of a full-blown snow hole requires several hours' work and much energy, but given good snow and stable weather the snow hole will be good shelter for days if necessary. Best prepared by two people, digging from two ends. Find a good slope or bank of snow, such as a deep drift. About 2-3m depth should be sufficient. Start digging two holes into the bank, about 2m apart. Once far enough in, turn inwards to meet in the middle. Block off one of the doors completely with snow and use a rucksack to block off the other when inside. Life is made much easier if a shovel or spade is available; failing that use a *deadman*. The ideal snow hole will have a ledge for sleeping on running along the inside. This ledge should be at a higher level than the rest of the snow hole, as heat rises. For the same reason, the door should be at the lowest possible level. A small ventilation hole may be poked out through the roof using an axe shaft. Once inside, the advantages of a snow hole over a tent may be realized. They are windproof, much

quieter and even slightly warmer.

In a real emergency it may be impossible to even attempt a proper snow hole but even a rough trench will help escape the real killer — the wind. If you can anchor a space blanket or other cover over the trench and so gain a roof then half the battle is won. As long as you can breathe it doesn't matter if covered by snow — it is a good insulator. In the morning you can wave a flag to celebrate life.

Snow ice. See *névé*.

Snow stake. Long, metal stake, often with a 'V' cross-sectional shape, used for belaying in deep snow. Due to its size and weight, the snow stake is confined to expedition use, particularly in anchoring *fixed ropes* in hard snow. Placed by hammering in as for a *drive in*, at an angle to the slope calculated to be at right-angles to the direction of pull.

Socks. Wool still reigns supreme here, with some nylon/wool mixes being perhaps the ideal for comfort, warmth and wear. Loopstitch socks are very warm and comfortable. With the introduction of better boot design most climbers seem to be wearing one pair of socks rather than the more traditional two. For rock climbing many crag rats dispense with socks altogether, obtaining a more direct 'feel' for the rock; thin socks are certainly better here for the harder climbs, with cotton being cool. **Tip**. For colder rock climbing where long socks with breeches are worn, try wearing ski socks — thin feet but normal thickness of upper.

Solo climbing. Climbing alone, with or without self-protection. Many climbers never solo, though the distinction between scrambling along an easy but exposed ridge and soloing a steeper but still easy route is a fine one. Obviously a mistake will be badly punished, which is why most who solo will do so well below their normal, roped level of ability. Solo climbing is certainly free climbing, unencumbered by the heavy paraphernalia and moving with a delightful lightness. In winter, it can be almost as safe as a roped ascent, given that one carries a portable belay in each hand while *front pointing*. However, the list of solo climbers who have died climbing is a sad one. Holds can break, feet slip, the nerve fail. Don't solo if tired, off-form, or otherwise distracted. It demands even more concentration than roped climbing.

Space blanket. A thin sheet of aluminium protected by nylon and used for insulation during an accident or in a *bivouac*. A development of the US space program, hence the name. It is remarkably lightweight and worth carrying in a rucksack as a matter of course. The very light sheets, with little nylon backing, are too flimsy and it is better to have the heavier model.

Speed. Slow climbers end up with few friends. While speed may not be very important on a small summer crag, on a long winter route it can mean much more. In speed we are not talking about climbing as fast as possible and forgetting safety. Much time can be lost, for example, by a slow and late start to the day's climbing. Almost as much time can be lost by an overcautious and fussy approach to protection and belays. In winter for example, bang in a belay and clip the ropes in using a *clove hitch*. Fast yet safe is the rule. Don't sit on a ledge for thirty minutes enjoying the view with your lunch —

eat it on the move or while your second thinks he's being belayed.

The other need for speed is found in hard rock, when the wall is steep, the holds small, and the arms weaker than you thought. In other words, there will be occasions when you have to make your mind up and simply go for it. Only experience will help tell you when and where. One of the interesting facets of climbing is judging your strength on a pitch, balancing your reserves against the rock to come, the protection found, being ready for the unknown. Experience is only gained by climbing.

Spindrift. Loose, unconsolidated snow found sliding down gullies and over buttresses in cold conditions. Frequently finds its way through climbers' clothing, and can make a climb anything from uncomfortable to impossible. Formed of small ice crystals and particles of crystals abraded from previously fallen snow. Can sometimes be seen blowing from the summits in bad weather.

Stance. Belay position, usually, if not preferably, a ledge. In winter it may be a footledge cut in the slope for comfort, in summer it is normally a natural feature which makes a convenient finish to a pitch or climb.

Standard. See *grading*.

Step-cutting. Before the introduction of *front pointing*, winter climbing involved the cutting of foot- and handholds using a single ice axe. The occasional hold may still be cut today while climbing, usually for a resting step or belay platform. Only a superperson or ego tripper will be able to completely dispense with steps. Hill walkers may also find it useful to cut the odd step, as being faster than putting on *crampons* for a very short stretch of snow. And we are all human and make mistakes — like forgetting to include crampons on a winter outing.

The adze is normally used, unless hard ice has to be cut, when the pick is employed. Modern adzes are designed for holding once driven in, and are not as efficient as older designs of axe are at cutting steps. The older adze is flatter, with fairly square edges, so that as the ice becomes harder the attack profile of the blade can be varied from using all of the edge to using a corner. On easy-angled snow one or two swings of the axe will scoop out a suitable hold. Too shallow a swing will re-move little snow, too deep and the blade will dig itself in, requiring wasted energy for removal. When cutting a step take several blows, with each suceeding blow hitting the slope above the previous one, so that you are cutting towards the cavity, mak-ing it easier to remove the next lump. Practice will soon show the way.

A zig-zagging ascent will be con-venient here, so that cutting steps, as any old-timer can tell you, is an ambidextrous game. When changing direction either cut a slightly bigger step for both feet, so that you can have a short rest, or cut the first step of the new direction.

As the slope steepens so will the line of ascent, so that eventually the best way is straight up the fall-line. Cut steps several levels in advance, but not so far ahead that you are leaning in too much to reach up, as your feet will then be in danger of slipping out. The step shape will change from being long enough to accommodate the entire boot, to being 'pigeon-holed', shaped to take the front half of each boot. The axe will then be swung in a more verti-cal plane. Holds will now need to be used both for feet and hands, so that

there will be two staggered lines of holds running up the slope, about 30–50cm apart.

Cutting in ice will be hard work, and one must look for any alternative before starting. To be in such a situa-tion without crampons suggests a serious error — should you not have abseiled out by now? The pick may have to come into action. As it is swung into the ice give the shaft a jerk away from the slope, this will help break away the ice. Ice may frac-ture in an unhelpful way. Make a horizontal blow or two first, then strike down above this manufactured weakness.

Most difficult of all, and a climber's nightmare, is having to cut steps for descent. Everything feels wrong; balance is important yet awkward, less force can be put into each blow of the axe, you find it difficult to reach far down. Only two steps at a time can be cut. Make them directly below, standing side on to the slope, with the rear hold below the front one. Step down as though descend-ing a ladder, which, in effect, you are. If you feel that the steps are inade-quate for the next person, who may have to descend without any protec-tion assuming a roped party, then improve the steps above you before stepping down. Take care that the steps are good enough; the position is difficult and the instinct is to rush. For very short sections of icy ground, a few toe scrapes may be all that will be needed to reach safety. Time can pass very quickly while cutting steps, so keep one eye on the sun.

Step-in bindings. See *crampons*.

Sticht plate. See *belay plate*.

Stonefall. A hazard of any moun-tains, though some rock types are worse than others. Natural erosion ensures a plentiful supply of loose rocks on a face; ice, snow, wind and wet make them fall. Another source of stonefall is other hill users. Gullies will have more loose rock and more chance of stonefall than any other area of a mountain. In the Alps, *couloirs* are preferably crossed or climbed at night, when they are safely frozen. A *helmet* is worn as protection against stonefall, particularly in the Alps. If a leader accidentally knocks a stone down or hears one approaching the call is 'Below!'. An experienced climber then automatically shrinks in against the face, hopefully under an overhang, while a novice might look up.

Stopper knot. Used for tying off the loose end of a rope in a main knot. The double stopper knot is less likely to come undone. In use it should be tied right up against the main knot and checked frequently to ensure that it has not worked loose.

Stove. Small, portable cooking stoves are an integral part of *camping* equipment. They are also commonly carried when a *bivouac* is planned or expected, eg, in the Alps. There are four main categories of stove, defined by the fuel type used. Though some can be used in a tent during bad weather constant vigilance must be exercised to avoid disaster. Best if the tent has an extension outwith the main area where the stove can be bedded down on the ground yet still be sheltered from the wind, which would otherwise extract much heat and possibly blow the flame out.
a) Paraffin. These are classic stoves, exemplified by the Scandinavian makers Primus and Optimus. Commonly found in half-pint (284ml) and pint (569ml) sizes, they burn paraffin

which can be found anywhere in the world (slightly harder to find in the USA, where it is known as kerosene). The paraffin has to be pre-heated, using alcohol or solid fuel tablets, but once burning it produces a good heat very cheaply. Good for campsite stays, though paraffin seems to have a knack of ending up on your hands despite all precautions. With care, when lit it can be used in a tent. Too heavy and messy for bivouacs, however, and superseded by the following type.
b) Butane gas. Has the valuable advantages of convenience, lightness and clean operation. Gas burners, of which Camping Gaz is a well-known make, run on liquefied butane supplied in sealed metal containers. Some stoves, notably the Epigas make, have resealable containers, allowing them to be broken down between bivouacs; otherwise a cylinder is attached to the stove until finished. Probably the most popular type of stove for climbing. Instant lighting, clean. Disadvantages are relative expense of fuel, problems of disposing of spent containers (you should take them back down to dispose of properly of course), potential for accidents if an unfinished cylinder is leaking (closest thing to a flame-thrower and no joke in a tent then). Slower than most other stoves and particularly affected by wind, but fairly safe and can be used in a tent, (with care naturally). Butane is also affected by cold, making it even slower on a cold morning. An unused cylinder could be taken into your sleeping bag, but it is definitely not a good idea to snuggle up to an already started one complete with stove. Epigas however sell gas cylinders containing a propane/butane mix, much better for cold conditions and high altitude use.

c) Petrol. This fuel deters many due to its obvious main characteristic — high inflammability. If you are not deterred, it is a fuel which is readily available and burns hot and fast. More popular in the USA, where the MSR (Mountain Safety Research) gasoline stove is popular. There is also the risk of leakage; walking around with petrol-soaked gear is not the way to long life and happiness. The MSR Whisperlite can run on either paraffin or Coleman fuel (a refined, unleaded petrol).

d) Methylated spirits. Definitely a low-tech stove, this runs on either liquid meths or solid fuel tablets. Very simple and safe in use, their only disadvantage is the fact that meths stoves are slower than other types.

The design of pots used with a stove is your choice, though aluminium wins through its lightness. Non-stick pots are available, leaving less scraping to be done after a meal. If not using non-stick surfaces, be advised that leaving uneaten food in an aluminium pot is not a good idea. At the least you will be amazed at how fast the pot can be leached through by acids, and at the worst there is good evidence suggesting that increasing your intake of aluminium is not good for your brain cells. No point in surviving a climbing career only to turn prematurely gaga.

Stretcher. Device used for carrying and protecting the injured. Models designed for use in the mountains have to incorporate the conflicting requirements of lightness and strength. Some can be folded when empty so that they can be carried like a rucksack by one person. Skids are usually present, for convenient sledging down hillsides or snow slopes, and some can be fitted with a bicycle wheel for rolling along smoother ground. In cases of bad injury on a rock face the victim may be lowered while tied on to a stretcher; there should then be a headpiece for protection against *stonefall*. Carrying a stretcher is a tiring and exasperating procedure for which relief teams of volunteers are always welcome.

Summit. The highest point of a mountain, though not necessarily the objective of every route or climber. It may be that the summit lies close to the finish of a route, or be en route to the descent route, in which case it will be taken in during a climb. It may be, particularly with Himalayan or other expeditions, that the summit is the objective, following an ascent of some route. In general, the higher the mountain, the more difficulty there will be in attaining the summit, and the more importance there will be attached to the summit. Some summits have been named by the local inhabitants, some by surveyors, and some after the name of the first ascender.

The highest summit in the world is Mount Everest, in the Nepal Himalaya (8848m, 29,028ft), named after Sir George Everest, a Surveyor General of India. The Chinese name is *Chomo Lungma*, though this is apparently the district name. Many summits are marked by a *cairn*; in the UK there is often a concrete triangulation pillar, used by the Ordnance Survey for mapping. Apparently these will no longer be required and will thankfully be allowed to disintegrate, returning many a summit to a more original state. In the USA and other countries there may be a summit logbook, into which names may be added.

Sustained. A pitch or route with a level of difficulty which is relentless for most of the way. The term is subjective, though a four-pitch climb with three continually hard pitches, for example, would probably be described as being sustained, though it would be more usual to describe the route as having 'three sustained pitches'. At the smaller level, a pitch may have three or four or more sustained moves, all of which maintain the difficulty.

Swaging. *Chockstones* mounted on wire have the ends of the wire pressed together and encapsulated in metal for a secure join. Swaging also neatly hides the sharp ends which would otherwise create havoc with skin and gear.

Tape. Flat nylon tapes are widely used for belays, runners etc. They are made into slings by buying the desired length and knotting using a *tape knot*, or bought prestitched. Tape is either tubular or flat, with the largest size at 25mm wide and 2.4m in length having a breaking strength of approximately 2000kg. The tubular tape is softer than the flat but tends to wear more readily. One advantage to be gained by using flat tape is that its slightly stiffer feel makes it easier to slip down behind flakes and thread round awkwardly placed chockstones. Tape is also bought conveniently prestitched as *extenders*, for maximizing the placement of *chockstones*. It is cheaper buying tape as a length then knotting it yourself, as long as the knot is finished off properly and checked at intervals. For a beginner the price differential might outweigh the obvious convenience and finish of a prestitched tape.

Tape knot. The only knot to be used for joining tape ends together. Known as a water knot in the USA. Once the knot has been tied, tighten

it thoroughly by applying body weight. There should be at least 8–10cm of free ends projecting past the knot, and these should be constrained by adhesive tape, which will also allow your personal colour code to identify your gear.

Tarbuck knot. A sliding friction knot developed by Kenneth Tarbuck and used with *hawser-laid* nylon rope.

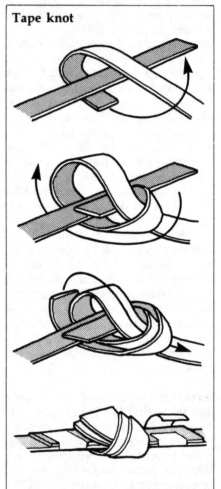

Tape knot

The only knot for tape slings. Finish off after tightening by body weight, by taping down the ends with your colour coded sticky tape, and check the knot regularly as it can easily work loose.

Under a shock loading it closes up, giving some degree of energy absorption in a fall. Now redundant due to the introduction of better ropes, and in any case not suitable for *kernmantel rope*.

Tension move. A technique used for crossing a wall where holds are scarce or absent. Involves leaning across with a taut rope running behind acting as a balancing aid. A series of such moves would be used during a tension traverse, which is very rarely required in the UK.

Thin. Climber's term for difficult, presumably originating from small holds giving technical difficulties.

Thread belay. A secure belay made by threading a sling through a hole in the rock then joining the two loops with a karabiner. A thread may be formed by a rock chockstone jammed in a crack, by a crack narrowing so that the two rock faces join for some distance, or, more rarely, by an actual hole in the rock. It is secure because it can resist a pull from any direction. Precautions to be taken are to check that if a chockstone is used it is jammed firmly and cannot come out, that the sling used is sufficiently long to avoid a three-way loading on the karabiner, and that the sling used will not pull through a narrow gap, perhaps one which has been concealed by mud or snow.

For some threads a kernmantel sling is safer as its greater diameter will not slip through a narrow gap. Threads which are difficult to arrange may be more easily set up if a karabiner is used to weight the end loop while dropping it behind a chockstone or constriction. Occasionally, a wire nut may be used to thread a difficult fixture, attaching a sling to the wire before pushing the wire

through the opening. As an interesting historical point, before the use of slings for runners, a leader would untie the rope and pass it behind a chockstone before tying on again, so forming a thread runner.

Through route. On some routes, usually gully climbs, a pitch will lead through an opening or hole, avoiding a steeper alternative. The opening is the through route. A narrow through route may require the removal of a rucksack, which may either be left for the second to pick up, or can be pushed through before passing through.

Thrutch. The meaning of this seems to have evolved from being a strenuous piece of climbing to being a strenuous and/or clumsy piece of climbing! What a novice may thrutch, an experienced climber *might* overcome more elegantly, but generally speaking a thrutch is a climbing problem for which there is no elegant or stylish solution and in which a climber is not in total control of the situation.

Topo. A photograph of a crag or mountain on which routes are indicated, usually by thick white lines which obscure much of the useful detail. The word is an abbreviation for topographical illustration, and though there have been some useful topos, most are no real substitute for a good diagram done by a climbing artist and backed by good route descriptions. Topos probably come into their own on the high mountains, where whole ridges or buttresses can be indicated by the dreaded white line (or white dashes), or black line if indicating a route on a snowy mountain!

Top rope. As used at present, nor-

Top rope

The climber in this illustration is attempting a steep crack problem, protected by the rope which runs up, through a belay at the top, and back down to the belayer, who is tied on to a flake belay. To prevent being lifted up in the event of a fall, the second might want to consider using an opposing belay of some kind, designed to take an upward pull.

belayer may wish to be tied on to a belay at ground level, particularly if much lighter than the climber, otherwise hilarious pulley effects may ensue. The belay should be set up so as to oppose an upward pull. It is certainly convenient to use a *belay plate*. The advantage of top roping is that no time is wasted with *runners*, in order to maximize training and (let us not overlook this point) have fun.

Tragsitz. A specialized harness allowing an injured climber to be strapped on to the back of a rescuer who is then lowered down a cliff face. Used in conjunction with a winch from the top for difficult rescues where a helicopter cannot be used.

Training. One very interesting change in climbing over the last decade or so is the widespread acceptance of training for climbing, just as in any other sport. Before about the mid-1970s, the main method of training was on the outcrops, though it always went under, and hopefully still does, the definition of fun. Most climbers still climb on the outcrops, though many do so more seriously now, to the exclusion of climbing elsewhere. In addition to the outcrops there are many other methods of training for climbing, some traditional, some new. As with other sports, perhaps the best way of training is to use a combination of methods, to prevent staleness and boredom. Before going into some of the training regimens, it should be stated simply that the best training for climbing, is climbing. See also *diet*.

Some of the more common training methods include: a) Running; b) Weight-lifting; c) Multi-gym; d) Artificial walls; e) Bouldering; f) Other methods.

The various advantages and disad-

mally a means of training on an outcrop by climbing with a rope running through a belay at the top of the climb for protection. The active climber will be belayed from the foot of the climb, so that in the event of a fall a short lower will regain contact with the ground, to rest and perhaps try again. With the fatigue of attempting a climb close to one's personal level will come the training effect. The

vantages of these are briefly dis-
cussed here. Please seek out expert
advice before considering any form
of exercise. There are now more
sports halls around than at any other
time. There should be sound help
there, while there are certainly books
specializing on most types of
training.

a) Running. Obviously this does little for the arms. What it does do is
increase the general cardiovascular
fitness — the heart-lung system —
so that endurance, so important to a
climber hanging on to a steep wall
climb, is improved. For certain areas
of climbing, notably in parts of the
world where there is some walking
to the climbing, running will make
the approach march much, much
more pleasurable. Think of walking
in to a distant crag with a rucksack
as big as your friends' yet being way
in front and not labouring. If that pic-
ture does not interest you then you
are a saint. For winter mountaineering the legs play a more important
role than they do in summer, so that
running will be beneficial. A rock
climber whose legs are not in shape
may experience the dreaded 'shakes'
while on an outcrop route, the jud-
dering, shaking leg motion which
can eventually promote a rapid separation from the rock. In winter, weak
legs may begin to let you down at the
end of a long day, so that what
started out as a fun day can become
a struggle.

Running fifteen or twenty minutes
at a stretch as few as three times a
week will produce beneficial
changes. If you are reasonably young
and into other sports already it will
not take very long to work up to this
modest level. If you feel you are seriously overweight or have some medical problem then discuss it with your
GP first. Long, slow running should
be the main aim. If your ego inter-
feres with your body's needs and
goes too fast too soon then injuries
will be the punishment. Listen to
your body. Avoid injury in the first
place by buying a good pair of running shoes. Not everyone can or
wishes to run on soft ground, so the
body needs to be cushioned from the
repeated shock of pounding a hard
road or pavement.

Once well into running you might
consider using your heart rate to
determine your optimum pace. We all
have a maximal heart rate, which
decreases slightly with age. It is calculated as being about 220 minus
your age. Whilst at rest measure your
resting rate. Now calculate your optimum running heart rate as being
your resting heart rate plus 75% of
the difference between resting and
maximal rates. One problem is taking your heart rate while running.
Get round this by taking it immediately after stopping!

Warm up before every outing,
doing a set routine of stretches with
perhaps some rope skipping or running on the spot to crank up the
heart. The warming up period
should last a minimum of fifteen
minutes. When stretching avoid
'bouncing', the outdated and potentially injurious style which can easily overextend ligaments which may
take months to heal. Stretching
should be like your running, long
and slow. Stretch as far as your body
wants to, and no further. See *yoga*.
Stretching will not only help prevent
injury during a run, it will be good
for climbing too. Warming down is
important too. After a run do some
more stretching before hitting the
shower. When you run is up to you.
Some prefer it early, some are on the
streets when everything else has shut
down and gone to sleep. If you run
at night wear something light or use
reflective bands, give the motorist a

chance to spot you. Try to maintain a fairly regular pattern.

Your first run might only be ten minutes, of which five might even be a walk. Who cares? In a few months you will feel very different. Your first route may be on the flat, but as fitness increases add some hills if possible, for variation and extra training effect.

Some climbers run to a climbing wall or crag, so fitting in two sessions in one. This will often mean carrying a small sack, which a beginning runner should avoid. What to wear is up to you, but start cool, just as in walking up a hill. In the summer months most will wear shorts and t-shirt, unless you feel you have really ugly legs or it is raining badly, when a thin nylon top might be more comfortable in cold rain. As it becomes colder some switch to track suit trousers, the thin stretchy type, not the house-lazing variety. Running in poor weather will not only continue to make you fitter, it will toughen you up for those wild days on the mountains. A final warning about running. It can become addictive. It is a healthy addiction, but one which you may find takes up more and more of your time. Some climbers switch to marathon running, finding there a challenge without the obvious list of penalty clauses owned by climbing.
b) Weight-lifting. This seems to ebb and wane in favour. It can be useful for generating power and strength, and also for adding some solid muscle where before there was little. As it is normally done indoors it is a suitable training regimen during bad weather or in the winter months. Before mentioning some specifics, we should differentiate between power and strength. Power is the combination of strength and speed, and is often required in sports, including climbing. Power = Force x Velocity.

Power is needed for endurance climbing, the ability to hang on for long times on steep ground, and for short bursts of power climbing to overcome a hard section dynamically. Most climbing will be of the endurance kind, more long-distance running than sprinting. Luckily weight-lifting allows the athlete to train differentially. Put simply, heavy weights with few repetitions of an exercise will develop strength and build tissue; lighter weights with more repetitions will build endurance.

As with any other training start modestly. Start also by consulting a trained coach, as it is too easy to cause serious damage by poor technique. Again, a sports hall will not only have a good range of equipment, it will have trained personnel who can even analyse your needs and devise a training schedule to fit them. Discuss climbing movements with the coach and emphasize endurance requirements. Read up on basic anatomy so as to understand your needs and the language of weight-lifting. Like running, the optimum for weight training is three times a week, or alternate days. This will be more intensive in the winter, if you are a rock climber, and can be scaled down as rock climbing increases. Stay strong over the winter and you will be ready to build on this in the spring.

Set weight-lifting exercises are broken down into sets, each of a certain number of repetitions. Commonly an exercise may consist of two or three sets, each of 5–15 repetitions. The aim is to begin with one or two sets and build up to three. For climbers, working for endurance, repetitions should be about 10–12 in number. The weight will be decided by your inability to properly finish the last repetition, and will be increased over the months as strength improves. As with other training, warm up before beginning. One of the best exercises does not even require weights — the humble pull-up. A good sports shop will sell a metal pull-up bar which can be adjusted so as to jam across the top of a doorway at home, or build one yourself. If you are already strong then hang a little weight from your waist and cross your legs at the ankles when you do your pull-ups. Do it with palms facing forward. If you were confined to one exercise only then this would probably be the one.

c) Multi-gym. This is really a variation on weight-lifting, involving, instead of the free weights of the former, various machines which incorporate adjustable resistances conveniently arranged using pulleys, cams etc. You perform an exercise at a machine, then either move to another machine or a different section of the same device for the next exercise. One machine may incorporate a good range of exercises, making it suitable for home use, given the pocket money and space. Some, like the Nautilus range of machines, do one exercise only, making a visit to a centre a necessity. The advantage a machine has over free weights is that it is more difficult to do an exercise incorrectly, and probably more difficult to injure yourself.

d) Artificial walls. Starting round the 1970s the need for indoor training walls was recognized. Considering the British climate this seems a belated awareness, but it coincided with the treatment of climbing, at least as regards training, as any other sport. Indoor walls can improve your standard remarkably, as well as maintaining a good level of rock fitness through the wet and cold winter months. They have several disadvan-

tages however; they are designed for the harder climber, they are ultimately boring, with a sameness of moves, no matter how well designed. They are easily and often crowded, though some climbers seem to be happy in a busy, noisy environment. They cost money. Holds will become unnaturally polished and slick with chalk. **Tip**. Take along a toothbrush for chalky holds. Finally, there always seems to be at least one thoughtless creature haunting each wall, either complete with ghetto blaster of incredibly poor sound quality and waning batteries, or some other antisocial behaviour. (If you take your training seriously then you should be concentrating on the interaction of body and wall.)

Most walls can be *top roped*, though as they are usually designed with the harder grade of climber in mind most climbing is done solo, unless the local authority stipulates that ropes must be used. Depending on the level of heating in the building housing the wall (though some walls are not in a building), the temptation is often to step straight on to the wall. Resist this as it will inevitably lead to injury. Warm up first with some stretching. Begin with an easier route. If possible try and climb down always, if need be first traversing to an easier line. Climbing down will work the arm muscles even harder. Many walls will have traverse lines, often just above the ground, so that the timid or tired can have a safe workout. Working out on a wall is more fun with a friend, who can watch your back on a hard move, point out eliminate lines, and make you try harder by the tried and tested methods.

The very fit and strong may consider wearing a weight belt of some kind on a wall. This works for some but the risk of injury becomes

markedly increased. Virtually everyone who climbs regularly and hard on a climbing wall will, at some time, suffer some sort of injury, even without weights. They probably increase your strength to some extent, but may do little for your endurance. In addition to the familiar list of shoulder injuries, broken ankles and wrists, strained groins etc, more chronic complaints due to overuse are beginning to show in the statistics. Forms of arthritis in the fingers, which now work much harder than in previous generations of rock climbers, have been reported in young climbers. You are warned.
e) Bouldering. It must be quickly pointed out that bouldering is much more than mere training. Indeed, for many climbers it *is* climbing. However, much fun though bouldering is, it is also one of the very best methods of training. It is natural and will improve natural techniques, giving an improved feel for the rock. When bouldering it is safer to go in company. Some committing moves are best done with a friend waiting to break your fall. Unfortunately bouldering does require dry weather, but on the other hand most boulders will dry quickly. **Tip.** Carry a small towel, pub-sized, to wipe and dry the soles of your rock boots. Try to minimize the amount of chalk you use, and keep it off the footholds whenever possible.
f) Other training methods. It is possible to buy or make fingerboards, basically planks of wood with holds on to which fingers can latch and from which you then hang. This will quickly induce injury (not to mention acute boredom!). Use them for pull-ups, so that the joints are working and the lubricating fluids of the body joints are circulating. Likewise, climbing up the underside of an overhanging ladder made from rope and wooden rungs (the Bachar ladder), is murder on your elbow joints. Neither of these techniques is for beginners. Chouinard makes a rubber ring for hand exercise, and there are several spring-loaded devices on the market for the same purpose. Both have an incredibly high boredom factor, though they are presumably used when it is not possible to do anything else. By repeatedly squeezing these devices, hand and wrist strength can be improved.

Finally there is the Bullworker. This is a neat device consisting of two metal tubes, one fitting inside the other so that it can be shortened by squeezing the ends. It will also allow itself to be shortened by pulling on strong cords attached to the ends. This is a compact isometric device, allowing a whole range or exercises, for all of the main muscle areas of the body, to be done in less than ten minutes. It is designed to be used daily. While it may not take the place of other body-building methods, if used properly it will certainly maintain, and even build up strength, with the minimum outlay in time and effort. It is worthy of consideration for those short of time and space.

Traverse. a) On a climb a traverse is a section where movement is made across the face rather than up. There are *girdle traverses* which can span an entire face or cliff, crossing other routes on the way. These seem to be out of favour at the moment. See *hand traverse.*
b) A longer expedition involving the following of a ridge and taking in several mountains. The greatest such expedition in Britain is the Traverse of the Cuillin Ridge in Skye, which involves the ascent of ten *Munros* over its 10km length. There are others, particularly in the Alps, with some involving *ski-mountaineering.*

Triangulation point. Shortened to Trig Point, this is a datum point, usually at a summit, used by the Ordnance Survey for mapping. Built of concrete or rock, the flat top has a brass ring where a surveying instrument can be mounted. Now superseded by satellite and other technology, these trig points will be allowed to weather gracefully away. Indicated on an OS map by a triangular symbol. In many countries beyond the UK wooden datum points have been used.

Tunnel. To dig through an overhanging snow *cornice* and so gain the finish of a winter climb. Obviously this has potential for disaster, so that one should be sure of conditions and the stability of the cornice before attempting such a technique.

Tying on. The attachment of the main climbing rope(s) to the *harness*. The knot commonly used for this purpose is the *bowline*, though the *figure-of-eight* is another one. Each harness has its own method of tying on, though most involve passing the climbing ropes through several strong loops then joining waist and leg loops with a *screw gate karabiner*.

Tyrolean traverse. A method of crossing a gap, eg, between two pinnacles, by sliding along a rope suspended from either end of the gap. The name derives from the South Tyrol, where spectacular pinnacles in the Dolomites sometimes required the technique. Though very rarely needed, it can be very useful for access to certain *sea stacks*. When climbing the Old Man of Stoer in North West Scotland, for example, a water channel has to be crossed. This is just possible at low tide, but during the climbing of the stack the tide will have come in, blocking off retreat to the mainland.

The answer is to fix a long rope (60m) across the gap in a continuous loop, leaving a sling on the stack side belay. The climber then hangs from the rope with a *screw gate karabiner* connecting rope and harness, and slides along the rope by pulling. For safety, there should be a safety rope attached to each climber and held by a belayer, so that in the event of difficulties it will be easy to pull the climber back to a belay. If the Tyrolean traverse is sloping badly an *ascender* or *prusik knot* may be needed to maintain position on the rope.

Vegetation. Pure rock climbing has only one place for vegetation, the tree belay. The Lake District of Cumbria is especially noteworthy for having so many useful trees on routes, providing *runners* and belays. Other areas, such as Scotland, have too much bad weather and wind for trees to have made much impact on rock climbing protection. Other vegetation, grass, moss, lichen, heather etc, is regarded as a nuisance, obscuring holds, retaining moisture. Vegetation is often removed while cleaning on a *first ascent*, but we should bear in mind conservation too, and keep this activity to the bare minimum for climbing. While a conservationist would argue that to remove any vegetation is wrong, a climber could reply that as vegetation breaks down the rock, hastening the processes of erosion, to remove some vegetation from a cliff is helping to maintain the integrity of the rock! Try not to grab for a 'green hold' if in trouble on a climb. While we have all used such last-gasp tactics on occasion, the plants often have shallow roots, and will not be very reliable.

In winter climbing, frozen vegetation is often one of the best materials for using with the picks. Many a *mixed route* would be much more

Undercut

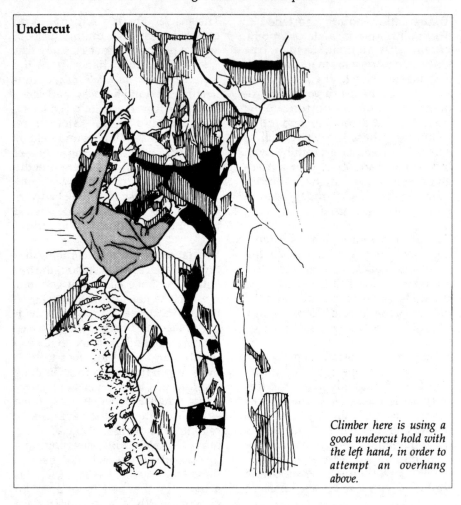

Climber here is using a good undercut hold with the left hand, in order to attempt an overhang above.

difficult, if not impossible, without frozen turf.

Verglas. Thin, transparent coating of *water ice* on rocks. Translates as 'glass ice'. Can make climbing virtually impossible, and walking treacherous. Often occurs due to a fast freeze following rain or wet snow (the motorists' equivalent is black ice). If the verglas is thick enough, *crampon* points may be able to bite into it, at least on a sloping or flat hold, but by definition and occurrence it will be useless for *front pointing*. In the Alps and occasionally in Britain, verglas

may also be found in cracks and chimneys, amongst otherwise dry rock.

Vibrams. See *boots*.

Visualization. See *meditation*.

Waist belay. The standard method of belaying before *belay plates* were developed. Basically, the belaying climber passes the ropes behind his or her body, running round the waist. As the other climber moves, the ropes are paid out or taken in, by sliding them through the hands alternately.

The rope leading towards the moving climber is the active rope. The other hand is the controlling hand, which takes a single twist of the rope round the wrist, for extra friction and control in the event of a fall. Several important points should be noted in connection with the waist belay. Neither hand must leave the rope at any time during belaying. The technique assumes a sliding movement of the ropes through the hands. As with belaying with a *belay plate*, consider in which direction the rope will be travelling, and arrange the rope accordingly. In the event of a fall the hands clamp firmly on the rope and the controlling arm is brought immediately across the body, towards the other hand, thus increasing the friction and hopefully stopping any more movement. The waist belay, itself an improvement on the *shoulder belay*, has been taken over by the belay plate. It may occasionally be used, eg, for quickly bringing up a second on easy ground in winter, but with the *Italian friction hitch* and the *belay plate* being that much safer, particularly for a weak belayer, there seems little point.

Wall. A steep mountain face, varying in size from the very small to the very large. Normally a fairly integral feature, but can also be used for some more complex mountain faces, such as the great North Faces in the Alps, and the North-East Face of Ben Nevis. On the smaller scale, wall climbing implies the use of holds on an otherwise smooth rock face, with no chimneys or gullies breaking up the rock architecture. A wall may of course be overhanging. See also *climbing wall*.

Water bottle. This can be very useful for day outings in Britain, and strictly necessary for climbing in the Alps and other big ranges. It is surprising how much water loss is incurred in winter, even though surrounded by frozen water. What is important is the amount of water in the atmosphere — the humidity — and the amount of exercise being undertaken. Many climbers do not drink enough water during a day's climbing, as they feel comfortable and the pub is but a short walk away. Check the colour of your urine; the darker it is the more water you need and the more stress your kidneys are under. **Tip**. Use a 'dilute-to-taste fruit drink', it will be even better than water.

The anodized, aluminium bottles are very light and convenient for water, but be sure the inside is lacquered for such a purpose and you are not using an unlacquered fuel bottle. Normally water bottles are coloured. In many countries, particularly the warmer ones, it cannot be considered safe to drink running water unless it is boiled thoroughly or purification tablets are used. In winter you may wish to carry a thermos flask of hot tea or coffee or some other drink instead. Oranges and tangerines have a fair amount of water in them; just be sure to carry back the peel, which will not be eaten by wild animals (unlike apple cores), and will not decay readily.

Water ice. Ice formed by the freezing of running water, as opposed to ice formed by the thawing and refreezing of snow. Water ice is generally much harder than *névé*, but much less tough, which demands an explanation. Toughness, in a material, is the measure of how resistant the material is to the propagation of cracks. Cracks can be prevented from spreading in a material under stress by the incorporation of other materials, hence the toughness of reinforced concrete. With névé, there is much air trapped in the ice, in the form of many tiny bubbles. These bubbles can stop a crack from travelling any further, hence the toughness of névé as a climbing material. With water ice, on the other hand, there is a much reduced air content due to its formation, cracks can propagate faster and further, and the ice can easily shatter on being hit with a pick, hence *dinner plating*. Water ice is harder than névé, as your pick and tired wrists will soon confirm.

Waterproof clothing. Necessary for mountain use, whether *hill walking* or mountaineering. Consists of an *anorak* and either overtrousers or overbreeches, the latter ending just below the knees and designed to fit over the tops of *gaiters*. Material may be a neoprene-coated nylon, *gore-tex* laminated nylon, *oiled cotton*, or any of the alternative nylons which incorporate some design of breathable layer. The first-named, the neoprene, is waterproof but not breathable, so that condensation due to perspiration will be present. In winter, waterproof gaiters are usually worn. These can be needed in the Alps as well, particularly to prevent soft snow later in the day from entering your boots. See *anorak*.

Wedge. a) The now-classic shape of *chockstone*, of which the Moac was one of the first, being developed in the mid-1960s. The early wedges had flat faces; most now have curved faces which fit more securely in cracks, there being a camming action. Sizes range from about 4cm wide to less than 5mm wide in some micros. Common makes include Rocks, Stoppers, RPs, HBs etc. Some of the very small wedges are made of brass, with the wire soldered directly into the head.
b) Wooden wedges were commonly

used in the Alps for *aid* pitches, before being replaced by large American pegs called bongs. The wedges had drilled holes near the wide end through which a sling was knotted for a karabiner to be clipped.

Weight belt. a) Method of intensifying training on a *climbing wall* by carrying weights. Should be done with caution to avoid injury. See *training*. **b)** Penalty clause carried by an overweight climber. See *training* and *diet*.

Weight lifting. See *training*.

Wet rock. Usually avoided by modern climbers. Depending on the rock type the friction can be radically reduced by wet. *Schist* becomes virtually impossible when wet, for example, due to its thin coating of lichen, while *gabbro* and *granite* can be almost as good as dry when wet. Previous generations of climbers often overcame wet rock by wearing socks over boots. If caught by the rain, a lessening of friction may not be the only problem to deal with. The fingers may be severely affected by associated cold, losing feeling and strength. All crags have a drying-out time, the length of which depends on the time of year, weather, outlook etc. During the winter, some cliffs rarely dry out, while others may take a few hours only. Boulders will obviously dry out much faster than entire crags. During descent particularly, take great care with wet rock.

Whistle. Carried by many hill users for use in an emergency, when it may attract the attention of others. Its sound probably carries better than the human voice, and certainly with less effort.

White out. In poor light conditions, with falling snow or thick mist and snow on the ground, the horizon may disappear, ground and sky merging. This is extremely dangerous, as it is then quite easy to step off the edge of a drop. If stumbling about a plateau looking for the descent then consider roping up in such conditions or looking for a *bivouac* site, depending on the circumstances.

Wind-chill. The effect of low temperature is compounded by the heat-extracting effect of the wind, and the two in combination should be taken into account when considering the weather. Charts are available which show the effect of wind, giving an equivalent temperature for each wind speed. To give an illustration, a 20-knot wind at 10°C will be the equivalent of freezing point in still air, as regards heat loss. When the air temperature is below freezing and a wind is blowing, be on the lookout for *frostbite*. The good news is that winds of over 40 knots make little extra difference!

Wind slab. See *avalanches*.

Wires. See *nuts*.

Yeti. **a)** Mythical(?) anthropoid animal reputed to haunt high areas of the Himalaya. Large footsteps have been seen in the snow, though they may be accounted for by the effects of the sun. Natives report seeing the creature from a distance, while the search for the yeti has raised more than one expedition.
b) Make of *gaiter* which encompasses the entire boot down to the welt. Suitable for winter climbing and higher mountains. Do make a boot waterproof. Disadvantages are the high cost and short life, if used in climbing as opposed to walking. The zip, which is normally now found on the front of most gaiters for con-

venience, will be covered by a flap, held down by velcro fastening.

Yoga. A system or philosophy originating from India and including the practice of various stretching exercises or asanas. These improve strength, stamina, flexibility, balance, coordination and the mind–body balance. The practice of yoga could not fail to improve your climbing, but as with other forms of training a qualified teacher must be sought.

Yosemite lift. See *pulley system*.

Zen. If one wishes to be a true master of an art (surely in itself a contradictory statement?) then technical knowledge of the art is not enough. One has to transcend technique, so that in the practice of the art, in this instance climbing, the mind becomes attuned to the unconscious, having emptied itself of self. I have experienced two fleeting moments of zen climbing in the last twenty-plus years of climbing. Others will also have done likewise, though perhaps without labelling the experience as other than being 'on the ball', or, 'on top form'. The zen monks of Tibet walk up mountains holding their arms straight against their sides with clenched fists. This apparently focuses energy on the cardiovascular system. I do not recommend following this technique; these monks can walk for days without flagging and have, in any case, devoted their lives and every waking hour to the practice of this branch of Buddhism. If there is a place in climbing for zen, then it is probably in the harder reaches of rock climbing. *Yoga* will maximize your efficiency as a mind–body unit, zen will take it one stage further. The rock climber will no longer be aware of being a body pulling up on holds, but of one reality containing the climber and the rock. The distinction between the two, the body and the rock, will blur, so that moves will be, even if only for a heartbeat, effortless.

Earlier in this book, in the entry for *meditation*, there is a brief mention of visualization, the pre-performance imaging in the mind of a sequence of moves. When you climb at the same moment as you visualize, then you have attained zen climbing.